Songs in My Head

Songs in My Head

A Cancer Spiritual

JoAnn A. Post

WIPF & STOCK · Eugene, Oregon

SONGS IN MY HEAD
A Cancer Spiritual

Copyright © 2015 JoAnn A. Post. All rights reserved. Except for brief quotations in critical publications or reviews, no part of this book may be reproduced in any manner without prior written permission from the publisher. Write: Permissions. Wipf and Stock Publishers, 199 W. 8th Ave., Suite 3, Eugene, OR 97401.

Wipf & Stock
An Imprint of Wipf and Stock Publishers
199 W. 8th Ave., Suite 3
Eugene, OR 97401

www.wipfandstock.com

ISBN 13: 978-1-4982-0807-9

Manufactured in the U.S.A.   08/10/2015

Scripture quotations are taken from the New Revised Standard Version Bible, copyright © 1989 the Division of Christian Education of the National Council of the Churches of Christ in the United States of America. Used by permission. All rights reserved.

For my mother, Troyce Post,
and mothers-in-law Barbara Nieman and Patricia Nieman,
courageous in cancer and in all of life.

Contents

Foreword | ix
Acknowledgments | xiii

Overture | 1
Verse 1 | 7
Verse 2 | 17
Verse 3 | 28
Verse 4 | 40
Verse 5 | 47
Verse 6 | 57
Verse 7 | 65
Verse 8 | 73
Verse 9 | 81
Verse 10 | 87
Verse 11 | 93
Verse 12 | 100
Reprise | 107
Postlude | 117

Bibliography | 121

Foreword

IN THE COURSE OF three years I buried three friends who died of cancer. Each of them—Robin, Gene, and Karen—was my age and at a similar place in life. They had spouses who loved them, children who needed them, work to be done, lives full and rich. I ache with grief just writing their names. Among the many injustices and insults of their deaths is this: they died too soon.

Too soon. Too soon for what? Nowhere are we promised decades of uninterrupted, robust life. Death is the inevitable end of us all. Though most of us pray that we die in old age, vibrant one day and simply not waking up the next, few of us actually go that way. Yet when Death takes a child or a teen or a middle-aged person, we rebel. "Too soon!" we cry. To which the Universe responds, "Says who?"

I had not realized how deeply my friends' premature deaths had impacted me until it was my turn to sit in an oncologist's office, my turn to hear the word "cancer" spoken of me, to me.

I remember little of that conversation, except for my first quavering question to the oncologist. "Will I get old?" This skilled surgeon, a man whose diagnosis saved my life and a man who has since become my friend, gripped both my hands and said, "Yes, JoAnn, you will get old." It was then that the tears fell. Worse than the startling diagnosis of cancer was the fear that I would die of it, that I would not live to see my daughters grow up, that I would not live to celebrate a fiftieth or sixtieth anniversary with my husband, that the work I loved would go unfinished, that others would bear the debilitating burden of grief that I carry for my friends and for countless others who have died.

I considered myself an unlikely candidate for cancer. I often boast that I am the healthiest person I know, that I come from a long line of folks who live well into their eighties and nineties. So I was taken aback when, in the summer of 2012, I was diagnosed with a large ovarian tumor believed to be benign. I assumed I would bounce back from that surgery as I had bounced back from other modest physical setbacks over the years. Although I was too groggy from anesthesia and painkillers to fully comprehend the surgeon's queries, my husband later reported that he could tell from the doctor's questions that something was amiss, "something big" was at stake. That something big was the discovery of cancer of the appendix, a rare, usually terminal cancer most often found on autopsy.

As I get older, I give thanks for odd blessings. Like that tumor. Had it not been for the benign, unexplained ovarian tumor, the cancer likely would have gone undetected and advanced until it grew too late to treat. Had it not been for that tumor, you would be reading my obituary rather than the journal you hold in your hands.

Because it is so rare and because few live to tell about it, there is no standard treatment protocol for appendicial cancer. My gynecological oncologist consulted with the world expert on appendicial cancer and with a brilliant medical oncologist in our area to map out a treatment plan. In the space of a week, I was transformed from a hard-working parish pastor to a full-time cancer patient, plunged into a year of rigorous and debilitating treatment. The only reason I was able to tolerate the isolation and torture of treatment is that I knew I would survive. Had treatment been only a palliative comfort, which is the case for so many, I don't know how I would have endured. But my surgeon had promised that I would grow old, and I held him to that promise.

To further complicate an already complicated situation, a month before the cancer diagnosis, my husband, James Nieman, had started a new and challenging job in Chicago, one thousand miles from our home in Connecticut. Though we did not relish the thought of living apart, the offer was too amazing to pass up, so we decided to keep our primary residence in Connecticut for two years until our younger daughter finished high school. I would continue to serve my congregation, and my husband would commute home as often as possible. It would be hard, but we have a sturdy marriage and a deep commitment to our children, so we would be okay. We could not have dreamed that as he dove into that new vocational challenge, I would face a life-altering challenge called cancer.

We could not have survived that year of commuting and chemotherapy without the faithfulness of our friends and family. We had food when we were hungry, companionship when I was lonely, drivers when I could not take my daughter to school events or retrieve my husband from the airport. We lacked for nothing. And when the house was quiet and my mind was clear, I wrote. At the encouragement of friends, I set up a blog on www.caringbridge.org. That online journal kept me in touch with people all over the world who asked to be in contact and to hold us in prayer. Sometimes I wrote long essays about my experience of illness and treatment. Sometimes I was able to scribble only a couple of exhausted sentences as I stumbled to bed after treatment. And sometimes, when sleep eluded me and the wolf of worry stalked outside in the cold darkness, I wrote in the middle of the night to keep those howling fears at bay.

My life has always had a soundtrack—song lyrics and pop songs and hymn tunes that play softly in my mind. A wise friend once advised me to pay attention to those songs in my head, because they sometimes reveal the truth in my heart—the depths of fear, or of hope. I have found his wisdom to be true. Even while enduring chemotherapy and its aftermaths, I always had a song in my head. So I share with you here *The Songs in My Head*, the journal I wrote and hummed and scrawled as I prayed and crawled and wept through chemotherapy toward life.

I am well now, living in Chicago with my husband and serving as pastor of a congregation on the North Shore. Our younger daughter is in college. Our older daughter is pursuing her dream career and recently married. Our lives are again busy and rewarding. That endless chemo winter is long behind us—at times now it seems like little more than a bad dream. But people I love are still living and dying with cancer. People still struggle to make sense of the abrupt and unwelcome turn from health to sickness, from strength to weakness, from dream to nightmare. If you are one of those surprised people, know that you are not alone, that others have sung this song before you, have already walked this dark road. As you read, know that these words come to you as a song to sing, a hand to hold, a friend to accompany you.

Will I get old? I don't know. Only God knows the days and years assigned to me. But I live each of the days I am given with joy in my heart and a song in my head.

Acknowledgments

THIS IS A BOOK I never wanted to write, since it came as a result of a diagnosis of cancer and a year of treatment. But I look back on that long, unwelcome year with gratitude for the countless gifts I was given.

Too often, it is not until disaster or sorrow strikes that we know how deeply we are loved. That was certainly the case with me. But from the first hint of trouble, we were surrounded by the expertise, assistance, and love of friends and family around the world.

I was cared for by a remarkable team of medical professionals who advised and supervised every step of my healing process. I owe my life to nurse-practitioner Karen Sullivan, who first sounded the alarm, Dr. Phillip Roland, the gynecological oncologist who performed the surgery and pursued my diagnosis, and Dr. Michael Reale, the medical oncologist who oversaw my treatment. They and the staff members of Saint Francis Hospital, Hartford, and the DeQuattro Cancer Center, Manchester, were God's hands of healing in my life.

Though I was on sabbatical from my congregation at the time of diagnosis, the members of Concordia Lutheran Church in Manchester, Connecticut, ministered to me without hesitation. I am most grateful to Mimi Boxwell, Jan Salvatore, and Irma Vincens, who coordinated the congregation's care and who are dearer than sisters to me.

Because my husband often had to be away during treatment, my sisters, Mary Bower, Janet Greene, and Carolyn Bormann, my friend Joel Ley, and our neighbors Dennis and Anne Fanning as well as Mark and Carolyn Piechowicz and their daughter Megan kept watch over me when he was absent.

Acknowledgments

Our parents, Erwin and Troyce Post and Robert and Patricia Nieman, who have themselves dealt with cancer, carried us in prayer and love across many miles.

My husband and I promised our daughters, Clara and Madelene, that while we would keep nothing from them, we also did not expect them to abandon their lives to care for me. They were unfailingly attentive, even as they raced through their busy days. It was a great delight to know that they were happily pursuing their goals and dreams, bringing the world to me in my confinement. Being their mom is one of the great joys of my life, and the desire to be their mom for many years to come spurred me to health.

It is for my dear husband James that I am most grateful. Near the end of my treatment, we celebrated our thirtieth wedding anniversary in a small cottage on Cape Cod. I pray that we will celebrate many more anniversaries, each year celebrating that no matter what that year had brought, we faced it together, and always with a song in our hearts.

Overture

Not Yet
Wednesday, October 31, 2012
7:41 p.m.

When we plan, God laughs.

I was to have had a port inserted in my chest yesterday, followed by a first chemotherapy treatment today. However, we were in Chicago last weekend for my husband's installation as president of the Lutheran School of Theology at Chicago (LSTC) and got caught there by Hurricane Sandy, delaying our return home by two days. Even if I had been in Connecticut, treatment might not have begun, since the storm upended the hospital and cancer center's schedules as well.

The new plan is this: the port will be placed a week from today. The first chemotherapy treatment will take place the following Tuesday. Already, at the very beginning of this process, we are delayed two weeks.

Even though no one wants to go through chemotherapy, I am disappointed at this delay, anxious to begin the process, to start this new chapter of my life. Thank you for taking time to read, to pray, to comment when you are so moved. We continue to be grateful for your concern and kindness, for offers of "anything you need." At this point, we are comforted simply knowing you are there, praying for us, remembering us, encouraging us, reminding us that more life waits for us at the end of this journey.

The answer to my anxious waiting is "Not yet." So I wait a little longer, planning to see friends and to continue healing after surgery, now six weeks past. I will enter chemotherapy strong in body and spirit.

Thanks for your care. It means more than you can know.

Homebound

Thursday, November 8, 2012
9:07 a.m.

WE ARE HOMEBOUND TODAY, thanks to the season's first nor'easter and a thick blanket of sloppy snow on the ground. The dogs are sacked out in their usual retreats—Ginger the golden retriever behind a chair in the office, Maggie the English setter on a corner of the couch. My high school-aged daughter is still sound asleep, since school was cancelled. I don't mind being homebound on snowy days like this.

We took the next step in my journey toward health yesterday. A port was installed in my chest—a simple procedure at the local hospital that will make infusions and other medical procedures easier in the next months. My left shoulder is sore from the procedure, but that discomfort will pass quickly. In fact, it will be all healed just in time for the first chemo treatment on Tuesday.

Here's something I'm thinking about: I've been in conversation with friends and colleagues about how to regard this new season in my life, wondering what image(s) will carry me through this unexpected life change. I am uncomfortable with militaristic images of "battling" and "surviving," though those images have been important to others. One of the oncology nurses suggested that I think about the chemotherapy as "sunshine in my veins, driving the darkness away." Again, it is useful for some but doesn't work for me (especially in a Connecticut winter). The pragmatist in me wants to say, "This is my work now," but that seems a bit too cold and matter-of-fact for what is a life-altering event.

My dear friend Herbert has offered "befriending" as a metaphor, suggesting I make peace with this treatment and embrace this time of healing as a welcome friend. I'm trying to make friends with that idea.

My sister Mary, with whom I grew up cleaning house every Saturday morning, wonders about a "cleansing" image—saying I could imagine the therapy removing impurities, leaving my body clean and whole.

Perhaps the image will come more clearly once we begin treatment in earnest.

There is also some wisdom to be mined in a recent realization that my primary struggle with this diagnosis—this "disability"—is that it robs me of a core piece of my sense of self. That is, I have always taken great delight in making others' lives easier, in doing things that might ease a burden or bring a smile or open a door, and in being both a pastor and a friend. It's not that I'm a pathological pleaser. But doing for others gives purpose to my days, to my life. All I am able to do these days is read and pray and wait. And make cookies.

Now, instead of giving, I am receiving. Receiving an embarrassment of riches—cards and phone calls, love and support, food and prayers, concern and care from all over the country. I feel guilty for all the love and time showered on us, but I know what joy it is to do that for others, so rather than feel guilty, I am learning to receive it with gratitude. And I am reminded of the need to remember others whose lives have changed and whose days are long.

I have also been introduced to the frighteningly large cancer community. To meet them, to hear their stories, to see that there is life on the other side of treatment shouldn't be surprising, but it is, and it is ridiculously heartening.

It's time for this day to begin. My morning pot of tea is empty. The dogs are agitating to step outside. The wind outside is warming, and the snow is starting to slush. At the opening of this day,

I give thanks for you and to God for the blessings already poured on our heads.

Chasing Maggie
Monday, November 12, 2012
7:36 a.m.

With a sheepish glance over her shoulder, she was gone. Crashing through the underbrush, leaping over fallen trees, chasing the squirrels who taunted her daily from the tall trees. Maggie was in dog heaven.

Dear Maggie. She is an English setter, her long legs powered by a chest deep and broad. She was bred to hunt, to run, to chase. Instead, we have tried to domesticate her, keeping her on a leash, confining her to a house, teaching her to be calm and to walk and to mind. She tries. She really does. But yesterday morning in the crisp fall air, crunching through fallen leaves with the smell of deer and squirrels in the air, she could not help herself. She slipped my grasp and gave in to her true nature. Within seconds, all I could see was the leash flying behind my snow-white Maggie as she disappeared into the woods.

Our reliable golden retriever, Ginger, and I gave chase. I lost a shoe in a tangle of branches. Ginger pulled on her lead like a sled dog. We dodged trees and scrambled over brush piles and splashed through puddles hidden under the leaves. It was early morning, and I didn't want to disturb the neighbors by shouting, so in a strangled whisper-shout I begged Maggie to come back: "Come on, Maggie. Come on back. Good girl. Come home."

We quickly lost sight of her feathery white tail. We were no match for her speed. Limping to a stop, bending over my knees to catch my breath, I panted to Ginger, "We'll have to wait for her to slow down and come back." Ginger surveyed me with a skeptical brown eye. She knows Maggie as well as I do—Maggie wouldn't come back until she was good and ready.

If you've ever chased a delighted-to-be-free dog, you know it is a futile task. It is best to wait, to rest, to trust that she will find her way back to home, to safety, to love. Ginger and I did not have to wait long. Though we could no longer see Maggie, we could hear her running through the trees. Suddenly, with a frustrated "yip!" we heard Maggie yank to a stop. Her pretty pink leash was tangled in a leafless bush, her adventure aborted. Ginger and I set off again, running through backyards and over driveways, following the sound of Maggie's consternation. When we found her, Maggie was in a lather, panting, straining, hoping we would untangle her and let her run some more.

But the race was over. Retracing our steps through wooded backyards, we stopped to retrieve my fallen shoe and limped our way home.

Recent weeks have felt like that morning steeplechase. Things were getting away from us. We were being dragged into places we did not want to go. While Maggie ran for joy, for excitement, in pursuit of adventure, we ran into danger and fear and not-knowing. It was not just the diagnosis of cancer itself that yanked us off our feet. It was the urgent pull of tests and doctors and procedures and decisions that surprised us. It was the thick tangle of insurance companies and scheduling desks and disability claim forms that slowed us. Sometimes it was all we could do to stay on our feet, to catch our breath. We limped. We begged. We gave chase.

Tomorrow I start chemotherapy. It will be my work for the next six months. We have heard tales of both hope and horror about other peoples' experiences with treatment, but how it will go for me remains to be seen.

But the chasing is over. We have had time to rest, to pray, to think. We know this is not a race. It never was. We had allowed ourselves to be distracted by the pace of events, the unexpectedness of illness, the head-spinning rush of decisions that needed to be made. We have made peace with our current reality. This is our life for now. To heal. To wait. To rest.

We are no longer frantic or frightened or pulling at the leash. We have been comforted and encouraged and calmed by the hundreds of people—health care professionals, friends and family, neighbors and colleagues—who have waited for us to catch up, who called us to safety, who have reminded us of love, who have brought us, sometimes limping, back home.

Just now, as I was writing, a deer glided silently into our front yard. He was framed by the rising sun behind him, magnificent in the early mist—all antlers and muscle and strength. Though both Ginger and Maggie were sound asleep, just as the deer's feet touched down on our grass, they leapt into action. They barked at the front door, scrambling over each other to get a better look, slobbering against the glass pane, whimpering to be free.

Dogs are so easily lured into a futile chase, eager to pursue game that is bigger and faster than they. But we will not be. Not again. We are home. We are safe. We step now, not into danger or adventure, but into life.

Verse 1

The Song in My Head
Tuesday, November 13, 2012
6:50 p.m.

There is always a song in my head. Sometimes it's something useless like "Louie, Louie" or "Can't Get No Satisfaction." But this morning at o'dark thirty it was the hymn "O God, Beyond All Praising": "and whether our tomorrows be filled with good or ill, we'll triumph through our sorrows and rise to bless you still."[1] It's important to pay attention to the songs in your head—they sometimes speak a truth we cannot consciously name. And this morning, that was true. I didn't know how this day would go—whether the day would be filled with good or ill—but regardless of the outcome, there is always reason to praise. And I do. There is much for which to be thankful.

I'm home from chemotherapy. Jim is home from Chicago. Madelene is home from school. Our Clara was in contact all day from Rochester, New York, and will be home for a few days Thanksgiving weekend. The dogs are being dogs.

The first chemo treatment has been administered without incident, but it was a long day. I had blood work done at 9:45, met with the oncologist at 10:00, was in the "chemo chair" by 10:45. The infusion lasted only five hours today—less time than expected because they're waiting to add another drug in two weeks. They want to see

---

1. Perry, "O God, Beyond All Praising," http://www.hopepublishing.com/media/pdf/hset/hs_4462.pdf.

how I tolerate today's treatment. I came home with fluorouracil in a portable pump; the pump will be removed Thursday afternoon. A CT scan and a checkup with blood work are scheduled for next week. So this is quite a process—three days of infusions every two weeks for six months. It's a full-time job getting well.

The cancer center is an amazing place. The staff is kind and efficient. The space is open and non-hospital-like. Other patients who heard it was my first time made a point to stop by to chat, to tell their stories, to encourage me. (I must have looked a little lost.) My pastoral colleague Joshua spent time with me at midday—what a kind man.

As the day wrapped up, I was overwhelmed with weariness. I asked the oncology nurse if that was because of the drugs. She said, "No, it's relief. You're underway now." So, the exhaustion I feel is all the fear and not-knowing and "what ifs" falling away. It was wearying to carry that heavy load for so long. I'm grateful to put it down.

Andy and Irma, friends from our church, brought supper for us tonight. We were as warmed by the meal as by their love. There was a new stack of cards in the mail, lots of e-mails, and text messages. We are so loved—it brings me to tears.

As this day ends, I sing another song. A psalm actually—an ancient song. I close this day with Ps 139:1–3:

> O Lord, you have searched me and known me.
>
> You know when I sit down and when I rise up; you discern my thoughts from far away.
>
> You search out my path and my lying down, and are acquainted with all my ways.

And finally this, as I make my weary, fluffy-slippered way to bed: "The darkness is not dark to you; the night is as bright as the day, for darkness is as light to you" (Ps 139:12).

Thank you for putting that song in my heart, for carrying these burdens, for being God's gift to me—to us—in these last days. There are many uncertain days ahead, but they will each begin and end as did this one—with a song in our hearts and God's light in our darkness. Good night.

Verse 1

A Child's Memory

Wednesday, November 14, 2012
1:17 p.m.

I remember it the way we remember many childhood events. With some of the roughness smoothed away, details filled in where there are blanks, sense made of nonsense, a little haze around the edges. So whether the storm happened as I remember it is unknowable to me. Whether the storm happened at all—there is no way to tell. But this is my recollection.

Our five-bedroom farm house sat on some of the flattest, richest soil in the world. Across the neighbors' fields, we could see weather coming at a great distance. We were rarely surprised. But on this particular night, we were. It was supper time on a late summer evening, chores done for the day, the conversation mostly small talk. Dad sat at the head of the table with Mom at his left. My oldest brother, David, sat at the foot. The rest of us tow-headed Post kids arranged ourselves on a hodgepodge of chairs and benches along either side. How many were we then? Five? Seven? All eight? I don't remember. But I remember that suddenly a powerful wind hit the house without any warning. Mom and Dad exchanged a look. I remember the sound of chairs scraping across the faded linoleum and Mom hurrying us down the basement stairs. I remember being surprised that we didn't clear the table first—we never left dirty dishes sitting out.

Soon we were safe in the basement, watching the sky darken through the small casement windows in the foundation. The wind picked up; branches hit the house. We were all there—all but one. Was it me or another who softly said, "Where's Dad? He's not here"? All my Mom said was "He's outside. In the storm."

I imagine that if I were a farmer, I would not wait out a storm huddled in a dark basement twiddling my thumbs and waiting for the "all clear." I would do what I remember my father doing—standing on the front step, silently watching the wind threaten all he held dear. A strong Iowa wind can topple silos, unroof barns, wipe houses off their foundations, and scatter livestock in all directions. Though a farmer can't do anything about the wind, he can certainly stand witness as the winds blow.

Our house did not blow away. Nor did the barns or the silos or the livestock. The storm left branches and leaves all over the lawn and the farmyard, but otherwise we were untouched.

Why remember that long-ago storm today? Because I continue to search for an image, a metaphor for the changes that have blown up against our sturdy, steady life.

The steroids in the chemotherapy drugs mean that sleep is hard to come by after a treatment. So, though I am tremendously tired, I cannot sleep. Instead, I crawled into bed midmorning, the sun streaming across the duvet, both dogs snoring softly, and picked up a book. I read,

> He thought of his father standing in the barn doorway, peering skyward as a thunderstorm approached, while his mother shouted, "Gar, get indoors, for God's sake." That was how it was, sometimes. You put yourself in front of the thing and waited for whatever was going to happen, and that was all. It scared you and it didn't matter. You stood and faced it.[2]

Is cancer a storm? An act of nature over which we have no control? Could such a storm rob one of all that is dear? I suppose. Though unsettling, this storm my family now faces has not pulled us off our foundations or left us bereft. But I am captivated by the image of my remembered father, and of Edgar Sawtelle's fictional father, facing the storm as it approached. Perhaps afraid. Certainly uncertain. But with no choice but to stand in the storm as it blew through.

I'm living with that image today, through the fog of no-sleep and odd little side effects of the treatment, like sensitivity to cold and a strange taste in my mouth. I'll let you know if it lasts, if it holds strong, if "standing in the storm" accurately describes this current circumstance.

---

2. Wroblewski, *Story of Edgar Sawtelle*, 472.

Verse 1

I'm preparing to study texts online with my old buddy Joel this afternoon. In preparation for our conversation, I have been reviewing the readings for this coming Sunday and happened upon the assigned prayer of the day. Listen to this:

> Give us faith to be steadfast amid the tumults of this world, trusting that your kingdom comes and your will is done through your Son, Jesus Christ, our Savior and Lord.[3]

Tumults? Another word for "storm." We'll stand up to them all.

One Done
Thursday, November 15, 2012
7:03 p.m.

This afternoon at 1:10 I was disconnected from the chemotherapy pump, and my first treatment was officially over. Today was a harder day than yesterday—tired, emotional, aimless, just-not-feeling-right. I don't know if it was because powerful chemicals had been coursing through my body for three days, or because I haven't slept well in that time, or because I was impatient to be freed from the pump and the drugs. Whatever the cause, when I returned home from the cancer center pump-free, I crawled into bed and slept. I almost feel human this evening. Almost.

My hope is that in the next few days the medicine will work its way through my system, doing its magic as it goes. Is it naive to imagine that I will be more energetic then, in better humor, perhaps even my old self? I'll let you know.

I have a medical reprieve over the weekend. Then, on Tuesday, I have a nurse consultation and blood work. On Wednesday, a baseline CT scan.

---

3. Evangelical Lutheran Church in America, "Prayer of the Day, Lectionary 33," *Evangelical Lutheran Worship*, 53.

It has been so encouraging to know that you are sharing this journey with us. This has been a surprisingly isolating experience for me and, raging extrovert that I am, that has been difficult. Your presence reminds me that none of us is alone. Thank you.

So, I have little of a profound nature to share tonight, except that I am grateful to have crossed this threshold and grateful to be doing it in your company. One done. It feels good.

Provoked by Love
Monday, November 19, 2012
9:32 a.m.

I snuck out of the house yesterday morning to attend the early service across town at a Lutheran parish ably served by my pastoral colleagues Scott and Kathy. Though our parishes do lots of things together and we are well known to each other, I had hoped to find a small sleepy crowd, to be relatively anonymous, to hear the Word and share the meal and then get the hell out of Dodge.

My desire for anonymity is two-fold. First, since this is cold and flu season, I am trying to protect myself from lurking viruses. Second, I am easily provoked to tears these days, more so than usual. Others have warned me that sometimes worship is the hardest hour of the week because all the defenses we maintain during the week are gently toppled by song and Scripture and people who love us more than they should. I, however, would not be caught unawares. I would worship with dry eyes and a strong voice. I would be the model of stoic forbearance. If only.

The first person I saw was Sylvia, whom I have known as long as I've been in Manchester. She greeted me with arms extended and said, "How are you?" I did not cry. I was unable to avoid David and Joyce, who descended from the choir loft like angels on a mission. I hugged them too, but I did not give in to the lump in my throat. Marilyn sat next to me. She and I share a wryly bemused stance toward the world, so she was a safe worship partner. But it grew harder and harder to fight the tears. The folks in front of me turned and enveloped me in great hugs. Friends across the aisle waved and blew kisses. Another squeezed my shoulder as he scurried to his place during the opening hymn.

Scott opened the gospel reading in a way my quickly crumbling heart could hear, tying his thoughts together with brief reflection on that wonderfully dissonant phrase from Heb 10, "provoke one another to love and good deeds."

"Provoke"? The writer of Hebrews must have had a thesaurus in hand when writing. "Provoke" is a great word for the love I received yesterday. As are "pester," "poke," "irritate," "needle" and "nudge." Love would not leave me alone.

The floodgates finally opened when, during the exchange of peace, a touch on my arm caused me to turn toward another provocateur, this one bearing a prayer shawl and a hug. "Don't forget," she whispered, "we love you."

It was all I could do to stand quietly as I waited my turn at the communion table, to receive the bread without soaking it with tears. I hurried from the rail, grabbed my bag, gloves, and prayer shawl, squeezed Marilyn, and fled the scene. It was too much, this love. It pushed and prodded and clung and held and nudged and needled.

Jim and our daughter Madelene worshipped at our home parish later in the morning. They were later than expected getting home from worship. Apparently, they too were ambushed by love. I cried again as they regaled me with a long list of people who had expressed wisdom and concern and kindness and more offers of "anything I can do."

This love is almost more than I can bear sometimes. It overwhelms the worry and the self-pity and the fear and the exhaustion. It dispels the darkness, lifts the load, and reminds me that it is by and for love that we are made.

A new week waits for us—a full and blessed week. I'm having tea with a friend this afternoon, breakfast with another tomorrow. Blood work tomorrow. CT scan Wednesday. And then we give ourselves over to unadulterated thanks—even the federal government provokes us to love one day a year.

Thanks for provoking and poking and nudging, forcing love on us whether we want it or not. I guess it's what we do, we who are ridiculously and outrageously loved by Another.

The Parade of Horribles
Thursday, November 22, 2012
8:07 a.m.

I ran into Ryan at the grocery store Tuesday. Neither of us got our shopping done. Instead we dodged other shoppers and their carts in the crowded produce aisles while we caught up on each other's lives. More specifically, while he listened, eyes wet, to my recent story of unexpected change. We had not seen one another since my surgery in September, and much has changed since then.

Ryan is not only our friend, he is also our attorney. It was Ryan who first introduced us to the "parade of horribles" from which he protects us, legally speaking. The parade of horribles is that long list of things that can happen, either by accident or through malice, that require the protection and wisdom of an attorney. His illustrations of the "parade" are chilling horror stories of other clients who have endured legal nightmares. Contested wills. Complicated law suits. Life-altering accidents. Human sorrow, stupidity, and selfishness in all its variety.

I woke this Thanksgiving morning in my warm home, in this safe neighborhood, knowing exactly where my loved ones are this day. The side effects of the first chemo treatment have mostly passed, and I feel like myself. I thought of Ryan's "parade of horribles" and substituted today's "parade of remarkables."

It may seem a small and trite thing to call these joys to mind, but in a world that is often horrible—on small and large scales—to

Verse 1

be intentionally grateful is, in fact, a necessary exercise, a hope-restoring task, a small light thrown against the wall of darkness.

Here are a few of the floats in today's parade:

- Last night for supper we enjoyed Lu-Anne's homemade pasta sauce, so thick and spicy and tasting of summer sunshine it left us speechless.
- My aunt Amanda called yesterday to remind us that she prays for us every day. Amanda's prayers are significant—when she prays, God sits down and takes notes.
- Our neighbor Nancy rang the doorbell last night, bearing a plate of warm brownies and a hug.
- Our friends Carol and Phil brought homemade coffee cake and the first season of *Downton Abbey* on DVD to the door Sunday night.
- My colleague Paul called yesterday to say, "I'm coming for coffee Monday afternoon. I'll bring biscuits for the dogs too."
- We got a card from Eileen this week—one of the kindest women in the world, a woman who suffered her husband's death just weeks ago.
- The mail this week has been filled with cards. My e-mail inbox is stuffed, the Caring Bridge guestbook brims with wisdom and hope, and I can't finish even the simplest errand without being accosted by some kind person asking after our well-being.
- We celebrate "Vegetarian Thanksgiving" today with Madelene. "Meat Thanksgiving" will happen Saturday when Clara is home. Too much food—twice!
- A friend from Madelene's summer canoe trip in Quebec will be here for a (no)sleepover tonight.
- Many of the people who hold us in love have endured or are currently facing far worse trouble than we. That they have time and energy to care for us is humbling.

- Our local Food Share met its Thanksgiving turkey needs, though only at the last minute.
- A tenuous truce in the Middle East is a relief, but my heart aches for the citizens and soldiers of those and other tense and dangerous places.

So even though we have been introduced to a small bit of the "parade of horribles" in recent weeks, we continue to be pulled into a far more joyful and hopeful procession.

The "modestly horribles" will rear their heads again this week. I have a long phone call with the Social Security Administration Monday morning to discuss my disability status—they have already declined my claim once without even opening the file. Chemotherapy is scheduled for Tuesday, with the addition of a new drug to the mix, followed by the two-day IV pump at home. The side effects will return, possibly stronger. None of this is horrible, but I can think of ways I'd rather spend my time.

A friend called Tuesday evening to check in. She has marched in the parade of horribles too often—twice with life-threatening cancer. She was glad to hear that I was feeling good, that the small side effects of the first treatment had passed. But she is also frank to a fault. She said, "JoAnn, enjoy these days. There are harder days ahead." She speaks from painful experience; her honesty is a bracing gift.

As I write, runners in the Manchester Road Race are jockeying for position at the starting line on Main Street. Floats in the Macy's Parade are ready to roll. Long lines of cars on the highway ferry empty stomachs to bulging tables. And I'm enjoying this day, delighting in a long parade of reasons to be glad.

Verse 2

Do I Have To?
Tuesday, November 27, 2012
8:00 a.m.

In a couple of hours, I will be on my way to the cancer center to begin the second chemotherapy treatment. I was a mess all day yesterday—aimless, tearful for no real reason, on the edge of angry. I finally realized in the middle of the night that my difficulty stems from the complete disconnect between how I feel and what I know.

How do I feel? Mostly like myself. The side effects of the first treatment have passed. I am able to do what I want—walk the dogs, keep the household running, talk with friends, read complex novels, write coherent sentences. I have to remind myself periodically that I am in treatment for cancer.

What do I know? I know that the surgeon is quite confident that all the cancer was removed surgically. But I also know that the cancer I have has a nasty habit of recurring. I know that, because of my particular cancer and new understandings of its habits, I will probably be in treatment for the rest of my life. My oncologist said that I need to think of this as a chronic condition—like diabetes or heart disease.

What's the disconnect? The only reason I ever feel sick is because of the treatment. The treatment that is designed to eradicate any lurking cancer cells and forestall the cancer's return as long as possible. The treatment that protects my health and ensures, within limits, full and abundant life. The treatment that is tailor-made, carefully monitored and graciously administered by people who have devoted their lives to the care of cancer patients.

So, what's my problem, you ask? Chemotherapy sometimes feels to me like the castor oil some mothers used to force on children to prevent disease. It tasted awful. It went down wrong. It did funky things to digestion. Children avoided it, spit it out, ran away, begged for mercy. "But I'm not sick!" they wailed.

Yesterday I was that reluctant child. I wanted to cancel the treatment, run from the doctor, pretend none of this ever happened, go back to my life as it used to be. "But I'm not sick!" I whined to a friend.

Fortunately, a good night's sleep, conversation with wise people who love me, and your persistent and loving encouragement to "keep swimming" find me in a better place today. Today I am again on the path that leads to life. I am the beneficiary of decades of research and study, a support network of friends and family that circles the globe, and a sturdy working faith that reminds me that all our lives are in God's hands. This treatment might feel like castor oil sometimes, but in fact, chemotherapy is a gift.

It's time to start the day, to take a shower—a luxury I won't have again until Thursday night when the IV pump is removed. At the beginning of this new day, I give thanks for you. I pray that the difficulties you face will be not castor oil, but gifts from a loving hand, gifts that lead to life.

A Long Day

TUESDAY, NOVEMBER 27, 2012
6:40 P.M.

IT WAS A LONG day of treatment today—seven hours of infusion, followed now by forty-six hours of IV medication at home. There are new side effects already: even greater sensitivity to cold, thick tongue, hoarse voice, extreme fatigue. Nothing surprising, I guess,

Verse 2

but new to me. The oncologist assures me these symptoms are nothing to fear. Only perceptions, not physical realities, he says.

But it was a good day—three friends spent the day with me. The staff at the cancer center are good and kind people. Our friends John and Kay had a warm meal waiting for us when I got home from treatment. The best news of all is that the CT scan indicated there is no detectable cancer! What a relief. The treatment goal is to hunt down anything microscopic and prevent or postpone a recurrence. I can live with that.

Thank you for your prayers and concern. They mean a lot.

Mileposts
Thursday, November 29, 2012
2:30 p.m.

Somewhere in a box in our basement is a photograph of me standing at Milepost Zero on the Alaska-Canada Highway. It was my birthday. I was twenty-six years old. My husband and I were setting off for our first parish calls in Anchorage, driving a 1971 Mercedes-Benz 220 packed with the few belongings we would need for the trip. Everything else we owned was stacked in a container ship, barging its way to meet us.

The 1985 edition of *Milepost* magazine is in the same dusty box. It is faded now, stained with coffee and mayonnaise, torn in a few places. We lived with that magazine for a week on the road as though it were holy writ—following its wisdom about the best place to eat near Milepost 787 or which of the many hot springs on the way was worth a dip. We were never disappointed with the magazine's advice. Every mile was just as it was described. It was a certain gift on an uncertain journey.

I remember that as the numbers on the mileposts increased, the number of miles between us and our new home decreased. We celebrated when the miles still before us numbered only in three digits rather than four. When we passed the mile marker that said, "Anchorage, ninety-nine miles" we whooped and honked the horn. Everyone else on the road did too.

When we finally rolled into Anchorage eight days after we first set out, the car's fan belt was loose and whining, the bug screen was irredeemably clogged with insect carcasses, the car's interior was unbearably warm because the heater switch no longer worked, and we were all out of sparkling conversation and car games.

But no matter how road-weary we grew, how much dust we ate, or how many miles lay before us, *Milepost* never disappointed.

I have thought about that tattered old *Milepost* in these last couple of days. This second chemo treatment was far harder than the first. I have called the oncologist three times for advice and reassurance about side effects and time frames and, this morning, to ask, "Tell me again why we're doing this?"

My oncologist has been more than patient with me. He has driven this road many times with others. He knows that the road is a bit different for each of us but that some things can be expected or anticipated, some things can be modified and adjusted, and some things simply need to be endured. He and others who have traveled this road stand as mileposts for us now.

I'm leaving the house in a few minutes to drive to the cancer center to have the pump removed. If last time is any indication, I will feel better the minute the pump is disconnected from my chest port. And, if last time is any indication, I will be my old self again just in time for the third treatment. That's something to look forward to, don't you think?

Mileposts. On this trip, they still number in the single digits. Two days of infusions. Three anxious phone calls to the oncologist. Four days on the pump. A couple of really bad days and some sleepless nights. There are many treatments, many tears, many phone calls, many sleepless nights ahead of us.

But I'm reminded daily of something my uncle Art used to say at the beginning of a project on the farm. "Well," he would say, "we never have to do it *all* again." It's true. I'll never have to stand at Milepost Zero on this particular trip again. What a relief. And something to celebrate, though I don't have a car horn handy or even a happy whoop in me at the moment.

Thank you for traveling this road with us. For holding signs before us about what lies ahead and the promise of rest along the way.

It's time to be disconnected from the pump. Two down.

Advent 1

SUNDAY, DECEMBER 2, 2012

2:17 P.M.

EVERY YEAR ON THE first Sunday of December, Don appears at my office door bearing the world's biggest poinsettias. With a conspiratorial wink he says, "These are for you." With those words and a quick hug, he's out the door. In spite of my notoriously black thumb, his poinsettias last all season long and never fail to brighten even the darkest winter day. He has not missed a December Poinsettia Drop in seven years.

I hadn't realized it was the first day of December yesterday until Don drove up to the house. I was still in my pajamas and bathrobe, easing unsteadily into the day. Without a word, he started unloading poinsettias—three of them, enormous and lush—intending to leave them on the doorstep without disturbing us. But the dogs announced his presence, so I met him at the door. With tears in his eyes, he said, "These are for you." And then he was gone.

As a parish pastor, my life is timed by the liturgical seasons. Advent is the beginning of the year for me, a pensive, thoughtful, sometimes dark assessing of the way things are and the way they one day will be. I love this season, standing knee-deep in ancient texts, wincing at the dissonant longing of its hymns, cherishing the silence of burning candles and descending darkness. For the first time in memory, I will not be part of a congregation's Advent longing. We will mark the season at home, to be sure, but private observance cannot hold a candle to shared silence, prayer, and song.

This Advent's waiting will be different for me. I remember two Advents when I was great with child. I remember the traditions of the parishes I have been privileged to serve—liturgies and festivals and children's parties and vespers. I remember the faces of children who are now adults illuminated by each Sunday's Advent wreath and I imagine the children's faces in my parish as they light the first candle this morning.

This Advent, separated from public worship, I long for other things. I long for the chemo fog to clear. I long for the uncomfortable days to pass quickly and the good days to last longer. I long for daily word from you who love me more than you ought. I long for the day when my life will return to normal.

But until then, during this unusual Advent, I join you in song and prayer and longing. And I give thanks for Advent gifts already received:

Don's poinsettias required a rearranging of furniture, they are so large. One glistens with the richness of black emeralds, another is the flirty red of the cardinals in our woods, while the third is a delicious twist of red velvet and buttercream.

My friend Margaret, who serves as chaplain of a cancer center on the other coast, called Friday afternoon with wisdom and counsel borne of love and experience.

A friend arrived at the door yesterday afternoon with homemade *pfefferkuchen* and a hug.

Other friends brought a feast for dinner; we will delight in their generosity all week.

Neighbors knocked lightly on the door last night to ask if I was OK.

At the end of the day, my friend Mark e-mailed to tell me I had been missed while our altar guild set the sanctuary for Advent.

In fact, I lack for nothing. Sickness tempts me with selfishness. We have all that we need.

Verse 2

Advent reminds me that God promises so much more than we even imagine to ask—for all creation, not just for me. At a distance I will join the longing of all God's people for peace and shelter, for warmth and nourishment, for healing and wholeness. Though it is still morning, I will light the first of our Advent candles, knowing that many of you are doing the same—we are together even when we are apart.

Blessed Advent.

Chemo Dreams
Saturday, December 8, 2012
7:19 a.m.

I've been dreaming about chemotherapy this week. Early in the week it was something about broken needles and bulging IV bags. Two nights ago a stranger in a white coat was encouraging me to try a new therapy he had designed. And last night I dreamt that treatment was taking place in Dubai, that terrorists were outside the cancer center , and we were all in danger. It doesn't take a Jungian analyst to figure out what these dreams mean.

Here's something that was probably obvious to you but comes as a surprise to me: cancer and its treatment are completely consuming. I cannot get away from them, even in my sleep.

I schedule my life now by "good weeks" and "chemo weeks." I spent a lot of time on the phone this week making arrangements for things I won't be able to do myself next week. All the Christmas gifts are already wrapped and hidden away. I paid bills and balanced the checkbook last night so that I wouldn't have to do it while "under the influence" next week. All our conversations are about chemotherapy. Our meal times alternate between meals I make and the meals delivered by friends and neighbors. The mail is full of cards expressing concern and love as well as medical bills demanding payment. The clerk at the grocery store yesterday said, "I heard about your cancer. Know that you're in my prayers." My younger daughter and I have a list of Christmas errands to do today, because I won't have the energy to do them next weekend. The phone rings as often with friends as with calls from the Social Security Administration with questions about my disability claim. My white blood cell counts were absurdly low this week, which could make postponing treatment necessary, but the oncologist hopes I'll be good to go on Tuesday.

Everywhere I go, the cancer goes too.

It is so tempting to be sad, to attend to the sorrow as to a sick child. Added to the allure of despair is having suffered the Mother of All Colds earlier this week. And on a gray, rainy December morning like this, the pull to self-pity is strong.

But the disappointments and despair are far outnumbered by all the kindness we have received, the signs of hope that emerge in surprising places, and the promise of health and wholeness again. As Calvin once said to Hobbes, "The days are just packed."[1]

Here is a sampling of the last week:

I had tea with a friend on Monday and breakfast with another yesterday—delightful bookends to my week.

Our older daughter was home for a few days this week, a rare gift from a busy woman.

Denny and Karen sent a box full of (Hershey's chocolate) hugs from Cassville, Wisconsin. I laughed when I opened it—what a great gift. And so them.

Jeanne and Al stopped by with supper on their way to Advent Vespers Wednesday night. Steve came by for a cup of tea and a much-needed catching up afterward.

Jim's parents sent me sheep's wool seatbelt covers to protect the site of the chest port from chafing when I drive. What a thoughtful, practical, comforting gift.

Sarah, her life already over-full with a new baby, a busy toddler, and an impending move, told me that she prays for us every day.

---

1. Watterson, *Days Are Just Packed*.

Verse 2

Our friend Mark has offered to serve as chauffer this week by picking Madelene up after a school event and retrieving Jim from the airport at midnight.

Our neighbor Dennis is steadily chopping up and carting away the Hurricane Sandy debris in the woods between our houses. When I assured him that he didn't have to do it, he laughed and said it keeps him out of trouble.

Our neighbor stopped in to ask if it was OK to have the gutter cleaner coming to his house that day clean our rain gutters at the same time. Of course I agreed and asked to see a bill. But he winked and said, "I think if you buy one, you get the second one free."

Beth spent three hours kibitzing at the kitchen table with me over lunch. We cried for joy and sorrow both.

Bob the piano tuner was here this week. When I told him why I was home, he sat down on the bench and burst into tears. He is such a soft-hearted man.

Our neighbor Carolyn dropped off a fresh loaf of bread from the bakery on Main Street and stayed to chat.

I had long phone conversations with my brother Steve and sister Mary this week. My sister Carolyn called on her way to a weekend meditation retreat to say, "You'll be with me the whole time."

I stopped at the church office to do some photocopying and faxing and to see the friends who are also my church staff. While there, I got a crushing hug from Heather and caught up with Marion, who is patiently undergoing cancer treatment herself. Though she is losing her gorgeous gray hair, her good humor is intact.

Today I will write a note to my grade-school pen pal, Abbey, who has promised to stay in touch with me by mail as long as treatment lasts. It's my turn to write.

One by one, the Christmas boxes are being carried up from the basement and their cheerful contents distributed throughout the house, each accompanied by a story or memory.

In spite of my chemo dreams, the joys continue to outweigh the sorrows. The good days number more than the hard ones. This sorrow is temporary.

I didn't turn on any lights in the house before taking the dogs for their walk this morning. When we returned to the house, I flipped on a kitchen light and was greeted by a flicker of red from across the room. My mom and dad had sent an amaryllis bulb to us at the beginning of chemotherapy. They placed an identical bulb in the big front window of their house on the farm, hoping that our flowers would bloom at the same time. And today the blooming has begun. I wonder if they are waking to the same blush of life this morning.

This Advent, the prophet Isaiah promises rivers in the desert and flowers in the wilderness. Though some days the rivers run with tears and the flowers are barely blooming, we already know that promise to be true.

Advent 2

Sunday, December 9, 2012
10:04 A.M.

I'M JUST HOME FROM worship at our sister church across town. It's been a bracing morning.

I sat down to peruse *The New York Times* before worship, and above the fold on the first page was news from Guatemala, Egypt, and Syria. On the way to worship I listened to a news story from Eastern Europe about the paucity of trained medical professionals and medicines there. I settled into my pew at worship and reviewed the worship folder; it was filled with invitations to be part of projects for the community's homeless, grieving, and impoverished. The opening hymn sang of our Advent longing for peace in all the world, not just our little corner. And then, in the homily, my colleague Scott wielded the machete of the gospel to cut through the clutter and remind us that Christ comes to our world not so we can have a sentimental, self-serving holiday, but for the sake of the world's poor and needy, those unjustly treated and living in places of danger. I also could not help but think that the biblical prophecies of peace we read in this season were first heard by our brothers and sisters in the contested land we now call "Holy."

The world was tossed in my driveway this morning; it sang in my ear and then followed me home. I had to sit down when I got home, feeling a little weak in the knees.

Being modestly homebound is a dangerous thing—it tempts one to self-centeredness, to small-mindedness, to quick judgments, to thin patience and easy hurt. You start to think that the world revolves around your house, your sadness, your aches and pains. If you watch enough TV news, you even start to think that being greeted with "Happy Holidays" rather than "Merry Christmas" is a big deal, the start of a War on Christmas. Really?

I received Advent gifts this morning. The gift of perspective. The gift of a loving shake. The gift of humility. The gift of knowing I am citizen of a broader world, a world filled with needs demanding our attention.

My pastoral colleagues all over the country are doing hand-to-hand combat with John the Baptist in the appointed gospel for the day. And I light the second candle on our Advent wreath at home—a flickering witness to the power of God to light the whole world.

Verse 3

The Journey
Tuesday, December 11, 2012
6:39 a.m.

Sleep is a rare commodity these days. I don't know if it's worry, or chemotherapy, or middle age that interrupts my slumber, but, to quote T.S. Eliot, I "sleep in snatches" these days.[1]

Today we begin the third round of chemotherapy. I am a bit anxious—there is some danger that my low, low white blood cell counts from last week won't have rebounded enough to allow treatment, but there's nothing to do about that. If treatment goes forward, I know the side effects will flare again—longer and stronger than last time.

Actually, T.S. Eliot was one of my companions during the waking hours of the night, especially his poem, "The Journey of the Magi." Here's how it starts:

> A cold coming we had of it,
> Just the worst time of the year
> For a journey, and such a long journey:
> The ways deep and the weather sharp,
> The very dead of winter.[2]

---

1. Eliot, "Journey of the Magi," 68.
2. Ibid.

Verse 3

My musings about an appropriate working image for this unexpected, unwelcome time of my life have settled for now. After living with images of battles, befriending, cleansing, and facing the storm, I realize that this is a journey. At "just the worst time of the year." With friends I have spoken of "junctures" and "milestones" and "progress." Every two weeks, I prepare for a chemo week like planning to be out of town—working lists and making preparations.

Today is another step on this unwelcome, sometimes uncertain journey. But others have gone before me, many of whom did not have the hopeful prognosis I have. Again, from Eliot's magi muse:

> This set down
> This: were we led all that way for
> Birth or Death?[3]

As you know, sometimes I wake with a song in my head. This morning it was a prayer. Two prayers, actually. One structured, the other as much a wish as a prayer. Both about journeying.

As Jim prepared for his final interview at LSTC this spring, we started the day with this prayer: "Give us faith to go out with good courage, not knowing where we go, but only that your hand is leading us and your love is supporting us."

And as I woke this morning, the words on my lips were these: "Set my feet on the road that leads to life."

Today we take another step. Thank you for being companions on this journey. If I could turn back, I would. But the way to life only leads forward.

---

3. Ibid., 69.

Damn
Tuesday, December 11, 2012
10:42 A.M.

ALL THAT MIDDLE-OF-THE-NIGHT WORRYING was for nothing. I'm just back from the cancer center—my white blood cell counts were too low to administer the chemotherapy today, so they sent me home. We'll try again next Tuesday.

When the oncologist told me that between the low blood cell counts and the severity of my reaction to the last treatment, further treatment today was ill-advised, I had strong words. He laughed and said, "I know better words than that." I'm sure he does. And there may be opportunities for me to use them in the future.

I had hoped to put this treatment "in the rearview mirror," as my sister Mary had texted early this morning, but it's not to be.

The bad news is that this will extend the length of my treatment. The good news is that I'll have a "good" week this week and will be stronger for next week's treatment.

Enjoy this already-unexpected day. And thanks for your steady support.

Advent 3
Sunday, December 16, 2012
8:42 A.M.

I LOVE TO PREACH. It is one of the great pleasures of parish ministry. And besides, as I sometimes quip, I find myself fascinating.

This might be the first time in three decades of parish ministry that I am grateful not to be stepping into the pulpit. My colleagues—Christian, Jewish, and Muslim—this weekend meet the upturned faces of listeners whose eyes, ears, and hearts are full of the horrors of the massacre in Newtown, Connecticut. Twenty-six schoolchildren and teachers were murdered by a manically

Verse 3

troubled young man, and for what reason? What will they say, these contemporary prophets, armed with the Word of God and burdened by the realities of the world? This Sunday I fear I would have to throw up my hands and say, "I got nothin.'"

Here in Connecticut, it is impossible to get away from the tragedy still unfolding around us. Radio. TV. Internet. Conversations with neighbors. Talk at the supper table. Even in sleep, the tragedy crept in. I had visions of our president turned tearful "Dad-in-Chief," the face of one of the fathers whose son was killed, the imagined terror of children and teachers huddled in a corner waiting for the gunman to find them, and renewed debates about more guns and fewer guns and different guns. But when I woke, it was with a song in my head. Not an Advent hymn, but a hymn written by Henry Lyle, commonly sung at the end of the day:

> Abide with me, fast falls the eventide.
> The darkness deepens, Lord, with me abide.
> When other helpers fail and comforts flee,
> help of the helpless, O abide with me.[4]

The darkness is deepening. Helpers fail and comforts flee. The helpless are further harmed. But we light a third Advent candle this morning. Because even on a grim and tearful day, we trust that the Light shines in the darkness, and the darkness cannot overcome it (John 1:5).

Chemo 3b

Tuesday, December 18, 2012
7:51 a.m.

After an aborted attempt at a third chemo treatment last Tuesday, we're going to try it again today. Hopefully, my white cell counts will have risen sufficiently to warrant treatment. As much

---

4. Evangelical Lutheran Church in America, "Abide with Me," *Evangelical Lutheran Worship.*

as I hate descending again into Chemo Land with its attendant complications, I am grateful to be underway again. A few more steps on the journey.

Since the second treatment, now three weeks ago, most of the side effects of chemo have passed. I almost feel like myself. It's hard to accept that at day's end the sensitivity to cold, the sleepless exhaustion, the muscle pain, the terrible taste, the neuropathy, the light headedness, the general "ick" will have returned. And that for two additional days I get to carry my own personal IV pump around, pulsing life-giving poison into my bloodstream.

But my personal sorrow is completely eclipsed by the sorrow to our south, in Newtown. Two funerals yesterday. Six today. There is a photo of our usually stoic governor on the front page of the paper, sobbing as he recalls having to tell parents their children were not coming home from school on Friday. Just looking at the photo hurt my heart; there is no way to imagine his anguish or the anguish of the hundreds who grieve the senseless deaths of so many. So today I give thanks that my trouble is so small, so temporary, and so completely fixable.

I am also grateful for you, knowing that many of you carry heavy burdens of your own. This day begins with prayers of thanks for faithful friendship, for loving family, for a safe home and access to medical care, and for God's guiding us through even the darkest days.

Of Whom Shall I Be Afraid?
Tuesday, December 18, 2012
6:21 P.M.

TODAY ALMOST DIDN'T HAPPEN. After a three-week hiatus from treatment, my white blood cell count hadn't budged. When they told me that chemo might not happen, I burst into tears at the nurses' desk. I've never wanted something that I didn't want so much! But they consulted with the oncologist, who has decided to add a new drug to my regimen that will make treatment possible.

Today I had my regular six-hour treatment. I'm on the pump for forty-six hours. On Friday I start a five-day series of self-administered shots to boost my white blood cell count in anticipation of treatment on January 2. They were a little reluctant to start the shots. They usually wait until further along in treatment, but my case dictates a change to "usual." In fact, this might become a regular part of treatment for the duration—the oncologist will confirm that at the next treatment. And the shots come with their own unique side effects: bone pain.

Oh, joy.

I had wonderful visits from friends while in the chemo chair. At midday, my favorite rabbi dropped by. Richard is rabbi of the synagogue in Manchester and a wonderful colleague, friend, and counsel. We chatted for a bit, then he read. Actually, he sang to me from the psalms:

"The Lord is my light and my salvation; whom shall I fear?" (Ps 27:1).

One of the side effects of chemo has been an almost complete inability to pray, except for brief moments, in partial thoughts, with stumbling words. I am ashamed to admit it, since as a pastor I pray for a living. But words fail me; peace eludes me. This is a sad circumstance for me, and it is sometimes frightening. But I realized as Richard prayed the psalms that my prayerlessness may not be the problem I fear it to be. Because he is praying. And my Episcopal colleague Paul, who visited today, is praying. And you are praying. Jews, Christians, Muslims. Our Mennonite friends who say, "You are in our prayers, such as they are." Those who claim no faith community remember us in their thoughts, send encouraging notes, and never fail to love us.

I am humbled and comforted to know that even when I cannot pray, prayers continue. As the evening hymn suggests, "The voice of prayer is never silent, nor dies the strain of praise away."[5]

5. Evangelical Lutheran Church in America, "The Day You Gave Us,"

Near the end of the day, when only a few patients remained at the cancer center, a woman younger than I came in with her physician. Within heartbeats, two oncology nurses joined them. I was not eavesdropping, but I could not fail to hear parts of their conversation. The patient learned today that her cancer has returned, and there is nothing to be done. Nothing but comfort.

She sobbed. The physician and nurses turned away from her raw grief, tears running down their own faces.

I didn't speak to her, don't even know her name, but tonight I will remember her in my prayers, "such as they are." I ask you to do the same. Her tremendous sorrow is now added to the tragedy in Newtown and to sorrows known and unknown around the world. I was also reminded again that my sorrow is temporary, that there is life at the end of this trouble, that hope is high, even though the struggle is hard. Whom shall I fear?

Jim is out of town this week. Clara is but a text message away. Madelene is here, counting the days until winter break. A lovely meal was delivered to our door. A friend is coming to sleep over tonight and another friend comes tomorrow. The neighbors will check on me tomorrow to "make sure I'm breathing." Good friends from California are in Connecticut for the holidays and will visit me on Thursday. We are well-loved.

I'll sign off now, though bedtime is some time away. The expected side effects are starting to emerge, creeping up on me like mist in a horror movie. I'm twitchy-tired from the steroids—sleep may be elusive tonight. But I fear nothing.

"The Lord is the stronghold of my life; of whom shall I be afraid?" (Ps 27:1).

Evangelical Lutheran Worship.

VERSE 3

Strong Medicine
THURSDAY, DECEMBER 20, 2012
4:22 P.M.

As much as I was looking forward to having the IV pump removed this afternoon, I was more excited about a visit today from our longtime friends Phyllis and Herbert. We have been friends for more than thirty years, our lives intersecting and intertwining in ways we could never have anticipated when we first met. Jim and Phyllis now share the seminary president gig, while Herbert and I serve as devoted presidential spouses. They are in Connecticut to spend Christmas with their daughter and her family but found time to make a detour to Manchester to have lunch with me.

I've mentioned that being even modestly homebound makes one selfish and small-minded. I notice every ache and pain, worry about every new symptom. Having Herbert and Phyllis at the kitchen table was an amazing gift, an opening of my world. We talked about seminaries and mutual friends and family and illnesses and writing, and too soon our visit was done. Our time was cut short by my appointment at the cancer center, but their presence and love were strong medicine for me, healing for my soul.

It's probably my imagination, but I start to feel better almost as soon as the IV tubing is disconnected from my chest port. So now, in addition to having reconnected with dear friends, we celebrate being a quarter of the way through this chemo journey. We've completed three of twelve treatments. Tomorrow I start the "blood building" injections with their unique set of side effects, but I'll worry about that tomorrow. Me and Scarlett O'Hara.

When we lived in Dubuque, Iowa, it was a four-hour drive to my family's farm in Titonka. We marked the hours as we drove: It took one hour to get to Casey's General Store in Nashua, while Waverly was halfway home. When we skirted south of Mason City, we had one hour of the journey remaining, and from there we had lots of landmarks—water towers and shortcuts and familiar farms. I thought of that familiar drive today. We're only a quarter of the way on this chemo trip, only at the Casey's, but at least we're on our way.

While I am grateful for the medicine pumping through my bloodstream, I am even more grateful for the strong medicine of your love and encouragement. I need both—the chemicals and the community. Your companionship on this unexpected journey means more than you can know. After all, as they say, the trip is not so long if you travel with friends.

Advent 4
Sunday, December 23, 2012
5:11 p.m.

It has been a busy day here, an atypical day for the pastor's home on the eve of Christmas Eve. As we were leaving the house for worship, we received delivery of an enormous basket of flowers and fruit and treats from friends wishing us Christmas joy. Jim and I worshipped together at a Lutheran church across town, and we were later delighted to welcome my colleague Scott to our table for lunch. I drove to Glastonbury to see the faces of my dear friends Joe and Pat, whose home has been visited by cancer as well. Wendy and her daughter dropped off dinner and the world's best brownies. We had hoped to have a Skype conversation with my extended family in Titonka, Iowa, where my folks and five of us eight kids are celebrating Christmas today, but the technology failed us.

Somehow it doesn't "feel" like Christmas yet. Maybe it is because the ground is bare here, or because I have been so removed from the usual marks of the season, or because the promised peace seems so far away. Even tomorrow morning will be odd: I have an appointment with the oncology nurses at the very moment a young chorister thousands of miles away welcomes Christmas by singing "Once in Royal David's City" on the BBC. It may also be that in my mind's ear I was missing last Advent's hushed silence before our Minister of Music laid his heart into "Lo, He Comes with Clouds Descending." Chrismons quaked on the tree; the worn oak pews vibrated beneath us. When Richard's hands lifted from the keys after the majestic third verse ("Yea, Amen! Let all the earth adore thee!") with all of us sweaty from the singing, I believed that anything is possible—even peace on earth.

Tomorrow evening at sunset this Advent will end—the liturgical one, at least. I have come to believe that "Advent" is not just a four-Sunday season, but a word to describe any period of deep longing, of hopeful or anxious waiting. So, though this Advent is ending, other Advents continue. With many of you, I wait for healing and restoration to "normal." Others wait for grief to lift or simply to ease. We wait to be reconciled or reunited with loved ones. We wait for real peace around the world. And some among us wait for this life to end, to wake one morning soon in the presence of God. Advents, all of them.

There are so many rich texts and tunes to be savored in these last moments before the Christmas bells ring, but the lyric that has haunted me today is from Jaroslav J. Vajda: "Proclaim the birth of Christ and peace, that fear and death and sorrow cease: sing peace."[6]

With you and the faithful around the world, I pray for the end of all our Advents, for the cessation of fear and death and sorrow, and for the continuous reign of peace. Until then, we light candles in the deep darkness, we sing until our voices tremble into tears, and we trust that Christ is coming. Soon.

A New Year Challenge
Monday, December 31, 2012
4:13 p.m.

Who could have known, a year ago tonight, all that would transpire for any of us in 2012? I've always believed it's one of God's great gifts that we don't know what lies ahead. If we did, we either

---

6. Vajda, "Before the Marvel of This Night."

couldn't sleep for delight or wouldn't get out of bed for dread. As is true with you, our year was full of unexpected joys and sorrows. Jim's new position at LSTC was a gift we didn't know to ask for. Two weeks in Italy as part of my sabbatical were wonderful. Our daughters continue to delight. My parish work is challenging and rewarding. We spent time with friends and family. We expanded the deck on the house so that our summer scotch and cigar evenings were better than ever. It was, in almost all aspects, a wonderful year.

Except for the parts that weren't. Most notably for me, the sudden shock of surgery and cancer diagnosis and aggressive chemotherapy and disability leave. You would think I would have come to terms with all of this by now, but I'm still SMH, as my daughter would text: Shaking My Head.

I realized it's been more than a week since my last journal entry. It was mostly a good week. My Christmas Eve oncology nurse appointment was brief, and the news was good: my white blood cell counts roared through the roof as a result of the injections. Sadly, for only the third time in fifty-three years I didn't attend worship on Christmas Eve. Clara got home at midday on Christmas Day and the four of us lollygagged over gifts and dinner. I saw my gynecological oncologist the day after Christmas—the man who saved my life with his surgical skill and diagnostic diligence. All week we watched movies, played games, napped, celebrated Madelene's sixteenth birthday, ate too much, laughed a lot, and shoveled snow. This morning I had breakfast with a friend and, just as we were leaving, the owner brought us a beautiful piece of limoncello torte to share. "Happy New Year," he grinned. Though the sun was barely over the horizon and it felt a little Marie Atoinette-ish ("Let them eat cake!"), we dug into his sugary greeting.

Tonight will be a quiet night—Jim and I have never been much for celebrating New Year's Eve. And this year the thought of swapping germs in the Connecticut cold with a sloppy scrum of cheerfully inebriated strangers is even less appealing. Instead, we'll toast the New Year with a cup of tea while watching *West Wing* on DVD.

Verse 3

Here's what I'm thinking about as the old year slowly morphs into the new. In my ongoing search for images that help make sense of this twisted time in my life, I was intrigued by this image in a novel I read last week. These are the musings of a young confederate soldier marching across soon-to-be-lost Southern soil:

> The men of the 2nd Army Corps walked this way—it could not be called marching—leaning forward, dragging foot ahead of foot, touching the pack of the man in front, stumbling to slow down and leave space. Most men's eyes were downward. The key was to avoid tripping on exposed stones, which would mean falling forward under the weight of haversack and musket into the cool, greasy mud and hours of discomfort and prayer for the warmth of sunlight. Staying upright was the thing. Balancing and stepping and staying upright under the crushing weight of the war.[7]

My next chemo treatment is scheduled for Wednesday. It feels like a forced march. I hate, hate, hate the thought of the three days of chemicals that lie ahead. Tears of frustration come to my eyes just writing those words. *Grrrrr*. A friend teased that it was like having your wisdom teeth pulled every two weeks. If only it were that easy. Even though I know the treatment will be manageable and lovingly administered, that the myriad side effects won't last forever and this temporary trouble leads to health, and that we are loved beyond measure and blessed beyond words, I hate it.

So, just for today, in this calm before battle, I'm following the lead of that weary soldier. Balancing and stepping and staying upright. A worthy challenge for the New Year.

---

7. Hutton, *Perfect Silence*, 57–58.

Verse 4

Random Thoughts
Tuesday, January 2, 2013
7:20 A.M.

I'M UP AND FACING a day of chemotherapy, the first of three days of chemicals: one at the cancer center and two at home. I slept horribly last night, alternately fretting the day ahead and chastising myself for fretting. Here are a few random thoughts as the sun rises on this day, the fourth of twelve chemo treatments.

Christmas trees. We dismantled Christmas yesterday, leaving only a few traces of the holiday on the mantle. As we lugged the tree to the curb for recycling, I was reminded of a long-ago conversation with my mom. We were chatting in the farmhouse kitchen as the last of the Post hoard piled out of the house and into their cars after a family gathering. You should know that when all eight kids and their respective spouses, offspring, and the revolving pool of boyfriends and girlfriends descend on Titonka, the weight of our frivolity tips the earth on its axis. We practically need a parade permit from the town. Wearily, Mom sighed, "You know, I love to see you all come. And I love to see you go." I feel that way about Christmas decorations. But only the second part applies to chemotherapy—I love to see it go.

School buses. As our daughter Madelene waited at the top of the driveway for her school bus at in the dark of early morning, I told Jim about the small shelters some kids in my rural school district enjoyed on winter days. Families that had particularly long lanes from the house to the road sometimes erected outhouse-sized sheds by the road so their children could wait for the bus protected from the weather. Our lane wasn't long enough to warrant such accommodations, but I always envied those kids. Not the long walk, but the warm wait. Though snow and wind and rain roared around them, they had, for a brief moment, shelter from the storm.

And this just in from Walla Walla. Our friend Joel, who lives in a city that sports a federal penitentiary in a state that still practices the death penalty, wrote this morning to wish me well in "The Chair." Macabre. But I smiled.

I'll be glad to see this day go. I covet the shelter of your love and prayers. And "The Chair" at the cancer center is not as awful as the nickname would indicate. Thanks for walking this road with me. I'll let you know how it goes.

So Tired

Tuesday, January 2, 2013
7:22 p.m.

OH, SO TIRED.

Another long day at the cancer center has ended. But I was only there five-and-a-half hours this time rather than seven, since they are able to push some of the medicines faster than before. The good news is that they've figured out the right "chemo cocktail" for me. The bad news is that my white blood cell counts skate perilously close to too low, so on Saturday I start another five-to-seven-day regimen of self-administered shots to boost cell production. Between then and now, I'm on a portable IV pump that will get disconnected Friday afternoon.

Jim was with me all day—a great gift. Nothing speaks to the sturdiness of a marriage more than a full-day of parallel play during chemotherapy. He worked; I read; we shared a sandwich. Of this, strong marriages are made. And great stories.

In the middle of the afternoon my friend Saud visited. Saud is a prominent critical care physician, an internationally-recognized Islam expert, a respected community leader, and our cherished friend. He, Richard the rabbi, and I have done some interfaith teaching gigs—I am the weak link in that otherwise illustrious chain, but they find me amusing, so I get to tag along.

Saud looked me straight in the eye and said, "JoAnn, you will be completely healed. I am certain." He was not speaking as a physician, but as a man of deep and tested faith. I tried to tease him about his certainty, but he was relentless. We talked. We wept. By the time he left to return to his patients, I was also convinced. When people of faith like Saud and Richard and so many of you pour your love and prayers and support into our lives, I am convinced nothing is stronger or more powerful.

So, though I am completely exhausted, shaky, spent, fragile, achy, weepy, and unsteady, I am deeply grateful. God is so good. And you are kinder and more generous with your love than we could have ever imagined.

Let me ask you a favor. I won't be able to sleep well until the IV pump is removed two days from now. But if we are strengthened by one another's prayers, then tonight I seek to draw strength from your slumber. Sleep like crazy—deeply, peacefully, long, dream- and worry-free. Do it for me and for all those like me who find sleep a rare commodity, an elusive goal. As I lay awake in the dark hours, twitchy with steroids, I will take comfort in your steady zzzzzzzzs.

"It is in vain that you rise up early and go late to rest, eating the bread of anxious toil, for God gives to the beloved sleep" (Ps 127:2).

Good night.

Verse 4

Channeling Tim Conway
Thursday, January 4, 2013
2:04 p.m.

Readers of a certain age will remember the comedian Tim Conway's "Old Man" sketches on *The Carol Burnett Show*. I've been channeling that character for the last two days—scuffing around the house with hair akimbo in worn L.L. Bean slippers, droopy-drawer plaid flannel pajama pants, and a once-regal-now-ratty oatmeal-colored wool sweater dubbed the Sick Sweater I wear when feeling particularly sorry for myself. Jim says I'm "a vision."

But the IV pump was removed after lunch, and I can now celebrate the completion of four of twelve chemo treatments. We're managing the side effects more easily. I'm learning to give in to weariness without a fight. I get to shower! Already I feel better than yesterday. Small victories.

I realized, waking from my morning nap, that almost more difficult than swallowing the big diagnosis of cancer is managing the small disappointments that come with it. Without even mentioning my inability to work or carry on a normal life, each day brings its own small disappointments. Today's *New York Times* arts section was full of exciting museum openings, shows, and things to do, but I won't be boarding a train for the Metropolitan Museum of Art anytime soon. We've had to turn down two invitations to Epiphany parties this weekend—being in close social quarters during flu season would be the death of me. There is a parent event at Madelene's school tomorrow, but I can't go—three hours in an auditorium is more than I can manage. Sometimes even answering the phone is an ordeal. Caller ID helps me sort the "have to answer now" calls from those I can deal with later. Good food doesn't always taste good. I tire of tea, longing for the occasional but absolutely forbidden Vitamin G (gin and tonic) in the evening.

But, when I am able to shed the Sick Sweater and its attendant self-pity, I also recognize small delights. Two nights in a row, friends have appeared at our door with a warm meal and even warmer hugs. A friend dropped off a wonderful variety of frozen homemade soups to tide us over until she returns from Florida in a month. The dogs are delighted that I nap so much—Maggie curls up beside me on the bed while Ginger lies in a pool of sunshine on the floor, releasing a sigh from one end and a flatulent cloud from the other.

The house is wonderfully peaceful on these cold winter days. The bedside stack of books waiting to be read fills the sleepless hours. Our middle school neighbors Megan and Caroline took Maggie for a brisk walk around the neighborhood. A good friend is flying in this week to help edit some essays I've been working on. I take great delight in your messages and cards and expressions of love. We are well-fed, well-loved, well-cared-for. What more can one ask?

The countdown continues. Four treatments behind us. We're on the way. Thanks for counting the days—and the delights—with us.

By Another Road
Wednesday, January 10, 2013
9:34 a.m.

My pastoral colleague Bob, recently retired, came to the house yesterday for conversation and communion. He confided that I am first on his homebound list—of course I'm also second and tenth, since in retirement he no longer has such a long list. He read for me last Sunday's gospel reading from Matt 2 about the visit of the magi. As with most pastors, he and I have read and studied and preached this text a thousand times, but it is a veritable goldmine of wisdom, so we dug in.

Bob commented on the fact that the star the wise men followed was visible only at night, saying it is only in deep darkness that we see the light.

We talked about the literary brilliance of the text, the Greek tragedy-ness of it all, noting that the reader knows the trap laid for the protagonist, but the protagonist does not (i.e., from his birth, we all know that Achilles' heel will be his undoing, but he doesn't). In the same way, we all knew the wise men were camelling into a trap, but they did not.

Then Bob and I dug in to two painful realizations: the nature of the danger they faced and the road that finally led them home.

First, the wise men thought they knew the difficulties ahead—dangerous roads, cold nights, robbers and thieves, and the possibility of failure. But they did not recognize the greatest danger: Herod, the one who sent them on this ill-fated errand. They were prepared for every enemy but the most devious. I thought about that in the middle of the night, thinking that my current journey has revealed a danger far more insidious than cancer: the danger of discouragement. I am fortunate that once each chemo treatment is over, I slowly move toward strength each day. I am learning to talk and pray and wait my way through the side effects and the sadness, but the despair—the fear that this will never end, that all this trouble will be for nothing—is the greatest danger for me. The wicked power in my life, the danger that lurks just behind me, the evil king on this journey is named "Despair." It is a powerful force.

Second, and more hopefully, I take heart in knowing that, in spite of the dangers all around, the wise men were able to return to their own country, albeit "by another road." The trip to find the promised king of the Jews did not go as they expected, and the diaper-clad toddler King was nothing like they had imagined. Herod nipped at their heels every step of the way, his spies sending reports back to the home office on a daily basis. Had it not been for the infamous dream in which they learned of Herod's true nature, they would have kept to their original plan and traveled back to him, back to their death. Instead, they went home by another way, taking a longer, more circuitous route, but they went home. The last thing Herod's spies saw of the wise men was the rear end of a camel. Like them, I will return to my "own country" eventually. Back to health and daily work and the ordinary joys and sorrows that give life such richness. But not right away. And not easily. I am traveling to my true country "by another road."

Today is a good day, better than a week ago by a country mile, and tomorrow will be better still. And I have many reasons to be glad. I whupped Jim in a Scrabble game last night. Food is starting to have flavor. Peaceful sleep is returning. A friend is coming for tea. The snow is melting, and I am able to be outside for periods of time without bundling up like Nanook of the North. Tomorrow our longtime friend Joel flies in to visit, work on a collection of essays with me, and babysit me through the next chemo treatment. Most is well with my soul.

Thank you, again, for being companions and cheerleaders on this long journey. This camel is moving slowly, but it is headed for home.

Verse 5

Sisyphus' Stone
Tuesday, January 15, 2013
3:31 A.M.

POOR OLD SISYPHUS. ONCE the most powerful king of ancient Corinth, the Greek gods sentenced him to an eternity of rock-rolling—pushing an enormous boulder up a hill each day only to watch it roll back to the bottom at day's end. This barbaric, shaming, and pointless exercise was punishment for Sisyphus' hubris, a daily reminder that his cruelty had eternal consequences.

Sisyphus and I share nothing in common—except for that damnable rock. I am not naive enough to imagine that my current situation is punishment for anything. As Jesus says, "The rain falls on the just and the unjust" (Matt: 5:45). Cancer happens. But I have been thinking about Sisyphus these last few days as I prepare for the fifth chemo treatment. I have had a really good week, feeling strong and hopeful, able to think clearly and enjoy my life. My reward for the gift of these good days? Pushing the rock that is chemo back up the hill. Stepping into the cancer center this morning strong but knowing that I will leave it limping. Already tasting the chemicals on my tongue, anticipating the steroid twitches, grieving the weakness that threatens every ounce of my courage and resolve. A friend told me she can already imagine the claw marks in the concrete walk outside the cancer center —evidence that I was dragged kicking and screaming into treatment.

But Sisyphus had no one to comfort him, no hope that his rock-rolling days would end. I do. I am surrounded by good people who love me more than they should. The promise of a full life at the end of this journey is real. None of the sorrows of chemotherapy last forever. This endeavor is not futile. One day this heavy burden will be pushed aside for good.

It has been a good week. My bishop paid a pastoral call yesterday. A writing colleague and I have been editing this week—the kitchen table is littered with coffee cups and post-it notes and discarded drafts of my essays. Our friends Stephen and Karin dropped by the other night with homemade ravioli for dinner and the gift of Pepto Bismol-pink bedclothes that were all ruffles and hearts and fluff, not unlike Ralphie's pink bunny suit in *A Christmas Story*. We laughed until we cried (though the fleecey pink bathrobe is quite nice—if you keep your eyes closed). I talked to a friend's mom on the phone last night, a woman who has always regarded me as one of her own. She said, "JoAnn, I wish I was there with you, but I pray for you every day."

Best of all, we will be well-loved today, as we are every day. An old friend will be my chemo companion today. Others have promised to stop by to say, "hey." This day will end, not with a rock at the bottom of a hill, but with Carol at our door with supper and her enveloping Midwestern hugs. My oncologist and the nurses at the cancer center could not be kinder. Your prayers steady us when we falter.

In a few hours I'll put my shoulder to today's work. Thank you for your faithfulness, your prayers, your good humor, and your hope. This stone is not so heavy when we lift it together.

Verse 5

The Rock That Is Higher Than I

Tuesday, January 15, 2013
6:52 p.m.

I'm glad this day is nearly over. Side effects are returning. I'm so tired I can barely stand. Once again, in spite of the neupogen shots, my white blood cell counts skate perilously close to too low. So, after the pump comes off on Thursday, I start a series of seven shots on Friday, rather than the five I did last time. It just gets better and better.

In the few long, unpleasant days ahead, I struggle most to maintain perspective. These days do not last forever. My strength will return. Nothing that I experience is life-threatening. I am loved beyond reason.

It helps that we were fed well and lovingly this evening. It helps that, along with supper, Carol slipped PBS' *Call the Midwife* into my hand. It helps to know that if I stay hydrated and time my Benadryl just right, I might catch some sleep tonight. A good friend is staying overnight—just to make sure I'm OK while Jim is away.

Thank you, again, for sharing this unwelcome journey. I felt you doing some of the heavy lifting today. I was keenly aware of the prayers that carry us through these days. Here are the words that I will carry to bed with me tonight: "From the end of the earth I call to you, when my heart is faint. Lead me to the rock that is higher than I" (Ps 61:2).

I might have started the day with Sisyphus, but I'm ending it with the psalmist. There is a rock that is higher than I, a rock that provides shelter from storms and protection from enemies. Sisyphus' rock may be rolling back down the hill tonight, but I'm hiding in the rock that is God's persistent, unmerited love and concern. It's been a hard day, but still I give thanks. For the rock. And for you.

SONGS IN MY HEAD

Where Did the Day Go?
Thursday, January 17, 2013
5:00 p.m.

I HAD INTENDED TO write a note to you all immediately after having the IV pump removed this afternoon. Instead, I staggered into the house after my appointment at the cancer center and promptly fell asleep—my second nap of the day. When I fell asleep, the sun was shining and the house was bright; when I woke, the sun was setting and the house was dark. Where did the day go?

My reactions to the treatment have become predictable, but each treatment is a little harder than the last. This time, I'm mostly plagued with neuropathy and exhaustion. The other side effects—sensitivity to cold, inability to sleep, foggy brain, and too many others to name—have set in, but I'm learning to manage them. FedEx delivered the pre-filled syringes for the seven-shot series I start tomorrow. The shots bring their own side effects. By the fourth shot, my legs are as heavy as if I were wading into Long Island Sound as the tide is coming in.

I just e-mailed a friend about another matter and told him that normally at this time of day Jim and I would be sitting down to an end-of-the-day drink and conversation. Instead, my 5:00 beverage of choice during chemo is hot water. We know how to live, don't you think?

But we will be fine. Tired, frustrated, sad, and achy, but fine. Jim gets home from Chicago tomorrow. Madelene and I will putter in the kitchen making supper tonight. (Our dear neighbor went to the grocery store for me—negotiating the aisles is a little more than I can manage today.) Each successive day will find me a little stronger than the last.

I trust that as the sun sets at your house, you know the peace and quiet we enjoy in ours. Even on these difficult days.

VERSE 5

Counting the Cost
SATURDAY, JANUARY 19, 2013
5:14 P.M.

ANY TIME I DECIDE to feel sorry for myself and the uninvited trouble we face in our household, I hear of others who have also been blindsided and buckled by unexpected difficulty. A young family whose primary earner is unable to work because of cancer treatment. A woman my age undergoing her fourth round of chemo for cancer that will not be deterred. An elderly friend whose bones are crumbling, who can barely get around her own apartment. Another patient at the cancer center who speaks quietly about the financial calamity this illness has exacted on her family.

I think of them often these days as I while away the hours waiting to feel human again, almost ashamed of how paltry my sorrow is compared to theirs. Jim chastises me for comparing suffering: "Ours is bad enough." But some people do suffer more than others.

The cancer for which I am being treated is not life-threatening, thanks to its miraculous early detection during surgery. Treatment is growing increasingly difficult, but in ways we can anticipate and manage. Our marriage is long and strong. Our daughters are older, able to understand what is happening, and not needing the constant attention a younger child might. My work waits for me when I am well. We have excellent health and disability insurance as well as savings to draw upon. I am receiving world-class medical care at the hands of people for whom cancer treatment is not just a job, but a mission. Our network of support is deep and wide, far more so than I could have imagined. In other words, while cancer treatment is exacting a significant toll on us, we are more grateful than grasping.

But, regardless of one's station in life, the cost of cancer is enormous and cannot be underestimated. I recently learned that the price tag for just the chemicals used in my treatment will soon exceed $200,000. Tests, doctors, nurses, facilities, unexpected things—these are all additional costs. And there is no way to put a price tag on the intangibles.

In Luke 14, Jesus shares a pair of brief parables to illustrate the need to count the cost and show the importance of thinking carefully about following him before strapping on the sandals. After all, everything has a cost, even discipleship.

The first parable is about a man who has plans to build a tower. Jesus says, "For which of you, intending to build a tower, does not first sit down and estimate the cost, to see whether he has enough to complete it?" (Luke 14:28). Jesus then warns of the public ridicule that would ensue if the tower were abandoned half-finished. The second parable is about a king heading into battle: "What king, going out to wage war against another king, will not sit down first and consider whether he is able with ten thousand to oppose the one who comes against him with twenty thousand?" (Luke 14:31). The odds seem formidable to me, but I'm not a king. Or a gambler.

Count the cost.

At first blush, it seems Jesus is encouraging his disciples to be ruthless in their analysis. After all, if a builder didn't have enough money to build a tower, he wouldn't build it, no matter how much he wanted it. And if a king were outnumbered two-to-one in battle, he would wisely consider an alternative to certain and crushing defeat. But there is more to Jesus' caution than a simple pencil-pushing list of "pros" and "cons" or heartless assessment of dollars and cents, soldiers and saddles. Some things, like discipleship, might be worth any price, even the price of humiliation or defeat. But the would-be disciple needs to consider that price in advance.

I remember sitting in the oncologist's office the day he outlined his proposal for my treatment. As it became increasingly clear to me that this was not going to be a simple thing, that nothing in my life would be the same for a long, long time, I said, "And what if I don't treat this? What if we trust the cancer is gone for now and treat it later, when and if it returns?" He and Jim just looked at me silently. As soon as the question was out of my mouth, I knew what the answer would be. Even though my body and my finances and my vocation and my marriage and my parenting and my friendships and my sense of self and my plans and my mobility and anything else you can name would be completely upended, the cost of not treating was too high. It was exorbitant. It was outrageous. Choosing not to treat would, sooner or later, cost me my life.

So, we counted the cost, and we have chosen to pay it anyway.

These are the things I think about as I wander weakly around the house reading, napping, and trying to make sense of my current situation. At the risk of sounding like a broken record, I come away from all this feeling deeply grateful. And more conscious of those for whom life is hard, those who have to choose between paying for health care and for groceries, those who are in treatment but without the hope of a good outcome.

Tonight I pray that God will soften the hearts and minds of those who could make health care affordable for all. I pray for those who face illness and sorrow without the comforts of home and family. I pray for those who have to choose between harsh realities. I pray with thanks for you, who lighten our load, who share our burden, who are more precious to us than gold.

A Burdened Heart
Thursday, January 24, 2013
7:10 p.m.

I WAS DEEP IN a writing project this afternoon when the phone rang. I was ready to let it go to voicemail, but when I saw Joe's name on the caller ID, I had to pick up. Joe is the contractor who built our deck, installed storm doors, and does all sorts of other projects big and small around our house. We hadn't spoken since August, a month before my trouble started. I picked up, and he said, "I don't know why I'm calling. I have had a burden on my heart for you and needed to be in touch."

I said, "I know exactly why you called." And for the next half hour Joe and I talked about all that has transpired since last we saw each other. My surgery and diagnosis and disability leave and treatment. His blown-out knee from a fall at a construction site. Our shared belief that God is at work, even in this. As the call drew to a close, Joe said, "JoAnn, I hope you understand when I say that I love you and miss you. If you need anything—anything—I will do it for you."

His phone call was just one of the many unexpected kindnesses we have received this week. Each day, as I crawl a little further out of the pit, I am reminded that God is at work in all of this. It has been a remarkable week:

- Yesterday morning I ran into three-year-old Gavin and his family at breakfast. They and another Concordia Nursery School family called to me across the restaurant. I have not seen them since May, but their greetings and love and hugs collapsed the time we have been apart.

- On the coldest day of the winter I received a prayer shawl from the parish I served in the Midwest. It is beautiful, soft, and warm. But warmer still were the wishes from the women who had knitted it for me. Seeing each of their names on the card brought to mind all the joys and sorrows we shared many years and many miles ago.

- Our friends John and Deborah sent a beautiful gift of fresh fruit and the reminder that they pray for us each day.

- My colleague Richard the rabbi called to check in and tell me he will bring lunch to the cancer center on Tuesday. "Do you eat tuna?" he wondered.

- My colleague Paul spent time in front of the fireplace with me yesterday, talking church over tea. It was wonderfully normal.

- Our daughter Clara celebrated her twenty-fifth birthday yesterday. It's not possible. I remember the cold Alaska day she was born as though it were yesterday.

Verse 5

- My friend Irma and I shared fresh banana muffins and hot tea this afternoon.
- My sister Carolyn forwarded an advance copy of *Downton Abbey*'s 2013 Christmas show and a wonderfully irreverent card. (She has friends in high places and a wicked sense of humor.)
- I was able to do an online text study with my colleague Joel. Even though I'm not preaching these days, it is still a gift to work through Scripture together.
- Friends from the Midwest will be in Connecticut for Easter and wondered if there might be room on my dance card.
- I had phone calls from my aunt Amanda and my uncle Leroy this week. Though they carry burdens of their own, they worry and pray over me.
- Our neighbor Carolyn did some grocery shopping. Wendy offered to make a Walmart run for us. Megan comes over after school some days to let Maggie drag her around the neighborhood.
- Cards and e-mails come daily, full of hope and love.
- My sister Mary is flying out from Iowa on Monday to take care of me and play Scrabble.

Like Joe, my heart has been burdened, with both love and frustration.

These weeks between treatments are so emotionally and physically complicated. New side effects have emerged requiring new medication and cautions. Each treatment hits a little harder than the last. I told Jim that the greatest frustration is that I have to think about everything now. Nothing is simple anymore. I used to take it all for granted—eating and drinking and walking and writing and driving and visiting and thinking and sleeping and shopping. I can take nothing for granted now.

I told my mom on the phone Sunday night that the only system in my body that has not been affected by chemo is my hearing.

Any other system you can name has been compromised. It's like being possessed. In fact, just to torture myself, I took another look at the pages and pages of possible side effects that can come with my treatment. I have many of them, even some of the really rare ones. Get this: it hurts to cry.

Each day is a wild mix of joyful and painful tears, reasons to be glad and reasons to be angry, triumphs and failures, hope and despair, exhaustion and flashes of energy.

But then the phone rings, or the mailman comes, or the fog clears and I can write, or we eat delicious leftovers from a meal made by another. And I am reminded that all these burdens are carried on many shoulders, in many hearts. And then they are not so heavy anymore.

I start the sixth three-day chemo treatment on Tuesday. I try not to think about it because I hate it so much. But it will come. And I will survive. And you will carry us through again.

Joe is exactly right. God is at work. Even in this.

Verse 6

False Summit
Tuesday, January 29, 2013
6:45 a.m.

I spent the summer of 1982 at Holden Village, a Lutheran retreat center in the Cascade Mountains. It was my task as the registrar's assistant to greet each new group of guests as their bus rounded the last bend into the Village. Swinging on to the school bus wearing my summer "uniform" of flannel shirt, jeans, and hiking boots, I fairly sang, "Hi, I'm Jo Post! Welcome to Holden!"

Every day off, we went hiking and climbing in the Cascades. One hot afternoon four of us set off for a distant peak with twenty-pound packs on our backs and the promise of leaping into a secluded mountain lake as our reward. I was a little daunted by the prospect of the hike, since the highest peak where I'm from is the town's water tower. But my companions said, "It's nothing. This is an easy hike."

Four hours later, sweaty, bug-bitten, thirsty, and more-than-a-little-crabby, I thought I spied the peak up ahead. We hiked another hour, then another hour. That was the day I learned about the "false summit," the illusory mountain peak that is, in fact, only a rise, a bend in the trail. The mountaintop we pursued was still hours away, but I didn't know that then. They also didn't warn me about mountain lakes in June. The water was so cold that I leapt in and nearly went into cardiac arrest.

Songs in My Head

Naively, I have been imagining this sixth treatment, this "halfway through chemo" day, as an arrival of sorts, a triumph, a destination. As though it will be all downhill from here. As though, to borrow from an old joke, "I can see my house from here." But this is really just a false summit, a tease, a wide spot on the trail before a much steeper, sturdier climb. When this cycle ends on Thursday, six more cycles remain ahead, each one harder than the last. Jim teased that by the time this is done, they will have to haul me out of the cancer center on a gurney.

So, I've been dreading this day. But I woke to a prayer on my Caring Bridge guestbook from Lynette, who was praying for me as I slept. The first e-mail of the day was from Janet, whose kindness is calm and deep. My sister Mary is here to take care of me. I spoke with brothers and sisters, my folks and Jim's, neighbors and friends on the phone all weekend. Our friend John surprised us with supper Sunday night, and when this day ends, Candace will feed us again. Today I'll wear the prayer bracelet my friend Irene, who is also the dogs' favorite veterinarian, beaded for me. The support and kindness we have received on this long climb have been breathtaking, overwhelming, humbling, heart-stopping.

As you know, I always have a song in my head. This morning I woke to a Charles Wesley text:

> Dark and cheerless is the morn
>
> Unaccompanied by thee;
>
> Joyless is the day's return
>
> Till thy mercy's beams I see,
>
> Till they inward light impart,
>
> Glad my eyes, and warm my heart.[1]

Today we climb on. I couldn't ask for better companions on this journey. The sun isn't up yet, but already God's merciful beams are shining on this house, on this day, in my heart.

---

1. Evangelical Lutheran Church in America, "Christ Whose Glory Fills the Skies," *Evangelical Lutheran Worship*.

Verse 6

A False False Summit
Tuesday, January 29, 2013
4:41 p.m.

We had to abort treatment at the midpoint today because I developed a sudden allergic reaction to one of the drugs. Within moments of the first symptoms—itchy palms, flushed face, hives—I had three nurses and my oncologist at my side. They are really wonderful people; I couldn't ask for better care. The nurse said my reaction was not common, but that it can happen. So, of course, it had to happen to me.

The plan is this. I'll load up on steroids tonight and tomorrow morning before making a second attempt at treatment tomorrow. I report to the cancer center at 10 a.m. tomorrow for the second round of my sixth cycle. They really want to be able to use this particular drug because it works miracles. So we're doing everything possible to make this work.

If it works, they'll give me the pump tomorrow to be removed Friday. Then the five neupogen shots.

If it doesn't work, we're on to Plan G, or maybe H. I've lost count.

I was so disappointed and frustrated when this happened that I couldn't even speak. But we are receiving excellent, kind care. There was no crisis. We have options.

Here I thought the sixth treatment was the false summit. Now the false summit itself deceives.

I am so grateful for your prayers and kindness, your encouragement and strength. I'll let you know what happens tomorrow.

Songs in My Head

A Beer with Finnian
Wednesday, January 30, 2013
5:53 a.m.

After a night of vain attempts to wrestle sleep to the ground, I finally got up at 5:30 to face this day. I was feeling sorry for myself, unable to pray, unable to rest, dreading today's uncertainty and hard work.

And then I opened my e-mail to find a photo of Finnian, my cousin Marilyn's Portuguese water dog, seated atop a bar stool and drooling happily into a cold beer, mugging for the camera. I almost laughed out loud.

Marilyn's photo was followed by an e-mail from our friend Ed in Anchorage, "one oddball to another," he wrote. His greeting was followed by a note from Keith and Ann, friends from grad school days who are traveling and teaching in Cambodia.

So, as I swallow handfuls of pills in anticipation of chemo and pretend to read the paper, I will envy Finnian, downing a cold one on a hot Minnesota day. I will delight in the memory of lingering at Ed and Sandra's dining room table while our young daughters played at our feet more than twenty years ago. I'll relax into the remembered welcome of Keith and Ann's lakeside home, gentle Indiana breezes blowing off the water. And I will grip the hands of Leslie and Madison and Jack on the other side of Birch Mountain as they pray for me before they head out the door to school.

Thank you for all your kindnesses to us. Your encouragement, your tears, your prayers, your honesty, your friendship. I will be in touch at the end of day. Hopefully, still with reason to smile.

Verse 6

A Duel with the Rock

WEDNESDAY, JANUARY 30, 2013
2:54 P.M.

It is with great relief that I can tell you there was no allergic reaction to the drugs today. They had pushed over 100 milligrams of steroids into my system last night and today to prepare my body for the treatment, and the end result is that treatment was successful, though I'm feeling a little wild. Talking fast. Pupils dilated like a dope fiend. Ravenous. I might not sleep much for the next few days, but it is a small (twitchy) price to pay for progress.

What this means is that we can stay on schedule with both the chemicals and the time frame for treatment. I was so afraid of a delay or a significant change in plans, but all that worry was for nothing.

I'm on the IV pump through Friday. On Saturday I start the five-shot series to increase my white blood cells. The night before the next treatment, I'll take a massive dose of steroids here at home to get my body ready. Chemotherapy is becoming a full-time job, but I'm glad we can continue to move ahead.

No other news. I'm tempted call Dwayne "The Rock" Johnson, and challenge him to a weight lifting competition. With the 'roids coursing through my system, I just might win.

Thank you for your prayers and concern. Trisha brought supper and hugs to our home this evening. My sister Mary is here with me these days, and she has commented more than once that she can feel your prayers. My mom said a bit ago that she imagines an army taking care of me: soldiers armed with deep faith, good hearts, and great hope.

This long day is nearly over. It's time for tea.

SONGS IN MY HEAD

Pre-Prognosticating the Groundhog
FRIDAY, FEBRUARY 1, 2013
1:39 P.M.

I WON'T BE WAKING up early tomorrow to find out what Connecticut's Chuckles VIII, Punxsutawney Phil's New England cousin, prognosticates on Groundhog Day. I already know that there are still six sessions of chemo in front of me, and that will be true whether Chuckles sees his shadow or not. So, knock yourself out, groundhogs—I intend to be tucked deep into my burrow when you emerge from yours.

It's good to have this sixth treatment behind me. It has been the most difficult so far—four days rather than three, with the addition of steroids and their attending ailments. The steroids kept me wide-eyed and agitated, but they also masked some of the usual side effects. Now, as the steroids wear off, the side effects emerge. I am not sure which is worse.

My sister Janet quoted her pastor to me, saying, "All cancer is brain cancer." Its true—chemotherapy is a relentless mind game. Keeping perspective. Maintaining a long view. Acknowledging the difficulties without being overwhelmed by them. Enduring bad days with patience and good humor while being deeply grateful for good days.

A friend said, "You don't have bags under your eyes, JoAnn, you have steamer trunks." Apparently, the fatigue is showing. I find myself, again and always, grateful. For my sister Mary, who took care of me this week, and for our neighbor who drove her to the airport this morning so I could rest. For Jim, who is flying home from Chicago this afternoon. For our daughter Clara, who stays close even when she is away. For our daughter Madelene, who walks in the door every day after school with something witty to share. For friends and family all over the world who pray for us. For daily bread and a safe home and the promise of healing. For kindnesses too many to name.

Verse 6

When I returned home from having the IV pump removed to give the dogs a quick walk after retrieving them from the kennel, I remembered the text from Hebrews about being "surrounded by so great a cloud of witnesses" (Heb 12:1). We are surrounded, both behind and before, by witnesses to hope. Thank you for walking this journey with us. We have a long way to go, but we won't be walking alone.

It's time to sleep. Is 2 p.m. too early to say "good night"?

The Storm Is Passing Over
Saturday, February 9, 2013
3:59 p.m.

We have survived Winter Storm Charlotte, but only with the help of our amazing neighbors and an unexpected burst of sunshine. Our neighborhood got about twenty-eight inches of snow. The roof of the house looks like an alpine lodge. The dogs twirl in snowy circles, trying to find a way to relieve themselves in the drifts. We did not lose power, as had been feared.

When our older daughter was in grade school, she sang with the Dubuque Children's Choir. I have fond memories of a particular spiritual they often sang, "The storm is passing over. Alleluia!" It was really lovely, with their fluty children's voices in three parts, rising and falling like snow-covered boughs in a winter wind. I wondered then if those ten- and eleven-year-olds had any sense of what they were singing, of what it meant for a storm to pass. I wondered if they knew anything about the fear that comes before a storm, of how much work it is to dig out afterward. Mercifully, they did not have to. That is a parent's job: to worry about the storms.

One sad casualty of Storm Charlotte has been Jim's ability to get home from Chicago. He was supposed to arrive home Friday evening, but three flights in a row were cancelled, and just as he was about to board this latest flight home, it too was cancelled. It now looks as though he won't get home until Monday evening. This is a tremendous disappointment for us, but there's nothing to be done. He did, however, get to chat in line with Tom Bodett, a KSKA radio personality we knew in Anchorage who is now the voice of Motel 6 and a panelist on NPR's *Wait, Wait, Don't Tell Me.* A brush with greatness, so the day is not completely lost, I guess.

It has been a stormy week, chemo-speaking, as well. The allergic reaction I had during the last infusion reared its ugly head again on Wednesday, just as the steroids were wearing off. I'm now on three new medications to counter this new reaction, and they're pulling the offending chemical from my "cocktail" on Tuesday. The oncologist said they might try to re-introduce it slowly at a later time, but not yet. I was, however, able to get my first full night's sleep last night, eleven days after the last treatment.

What does all this mean? Nothing. Storms come, but they always go. It is true of snow and cancelled flights and chemotherapy. And even as the TV news anchors are debriefing this storm, they are warning of another coming our way early this week.

Storms pass, and even as they do, other storms are building behind them.

But our neighbors and friends dig us out, airplanes eventually take to the skies, our homes are safe and warm, chemotherapy works its destructive yet life-giving magic, and every storm passes over. I'm not yet ready to tack the "Alleluia" on the end of that spiritual, but I am grateful that this particular storm has blown itself out to sea.

Verse 7

Praying on the Phone
Tuesday, February 12, 2013
7:16 a.m.

On a particularly pathetic morning last week, my colleague from New Horizon Baptist Church called. Their congregation has found a home among us Lutherans, and though we don't worship together often, we support each other's ministries and enjoy each other's company.

Pastor Simpson called not to chat, but to pray. On the phone. I have prayed with people on the phone before, but it is not my preferred method—it's rather like kissing through a screen door. But Pastor Simpson is a woman of profound faith and not easily deterred. She quickly drew me into her outstretched arms and began to simultaneously pray to God and preach to me. It was clear she had bent God's ear about me before. No introductions were needed. She launched into a litany of requests: healing, courage, strength, protection, peace. Her bids were respectful but urgent—God was not going to get away easily. Her voice rose, and her words tumbled over one another. It was hard for me to keep up, but it was God who had to pay attention.

Then she turned her attention to the devil, who had been, metaphorically speaking, tiptoeing his sorry behind out the door and out of her reach. She grabbed him by the scruff of the neck, rebuked and mocked him and tossed him aside. She has no time for his dark mischief.

And then she praised. We praised. "Thank you. Thank you. Thank you." Six, seven, eight times. I lost count. I was sitting on our oak staircase, looking out the front door, clutching the phone to my ear as she prayed, the tears streaming down my face. "Thank you. Thank you." And finally, "Praise the Lord! Amen!"

I had a hard time sleeping last night, anticipating this seventh chemo cycle. Treatment feels like a slow leak in a tire—three diminishing days as the drugs take hold. Then more than that many days to recover, to sit up straight, to feel like me. But Pastor Simpson's prayer was still thrumming in my heart, so I lay in the dark and let her strong hands rest on my head, letting her words swirl around God's ears and our home. And I gave thanks.

Jim finally got home last night, with his plane coming in through fog so heavy I feared it could not land. Madelene's school was cancelled again today because of storm cleanup, so she will join us at the cancer center when she wakes at the crack of noon. Already this morning my e-mail and the blog guestbook are full of encouragement and kindness. So, we enter this unwelcome day. But not alone.

Yesterday morning, I watched out our front window as a snowplow labored up our street, followed by a salt-crusted Subaru Forester, followed by another snowplow. It was dicey business, since none of the vehicles had a firm grip on the street. On this icy Connecticut morning, I feel like that sandwiched car—your prayers and love are plowing the trouble out of the way and following close behind to catch us should we slip and fall. You give us great strength and hope. So I add another "Thank you" to the end of Pastor Simpson's prayer.

It's time for a cup of tea, a glance at the newspaper, and breakfast before treatment. I'll leave you with a word from a friend in Chicago, a friend who knows cancer too well. She wrote, "Looking forward to the day when you're drinking from the saucer, 'cause your cup has overflowed." That's worth another "Praise the Lord," don't you think?

Verse 7

All Things End

Tuesday, February 12, 2013
3:29 p.m.

We're home from the first day of my seventh treatment. We had a long conversation with Dr. Reale about what it means that I reacted so strongly to one of the drugs last time. He has decided it is not wise to reintroduce it. He's been researching options and has concluded that six full treatments with the oxaliplatin are sufficient if we continue with the remaining six treatments at full force (*sans* oxaliplatin). I'm holding my breath at this news because it is too good to be true—it was the oxaliplatin that caused most of the side effects and heartaches and sorrows. With that out of the mix, I already feel better than I usually do at the end of this day. Not as achy or tired or sensitive. Whether that feeling is real or simply the temporary product of my imagination, I'll enjoy it for now.

Jim and Madelene were with me for the day. Our friend Janet brought a bag of books to add to my bedside reading stack and will return to the house tonight with supper. Tomorrow my colleague Bill will bring ashes and communion to the house for us.

I have to remind myself that this is Shrove Tuesday, which means tomorrow is Ash Wednesday, since I'm a little out of sync with the liturgical year. But I've always loved Ash Wednesday for its honesty, its strong signs, and its stark message. And I've always been grateful for the ashes' reminder of mortality and the promise that all things end. Not only do our lives inevitably come to a close, but illness ends, and sorrow ends, and war ends, and hunger ends, and anger ends, and chemotherapy ends, and all those things that make our lives so dark. They all come to an end. Sometimes when Jim or I face a particularly awful day, we say to one another, "All days end, eventually. This one will too." It's a comfort, actually. To know that all things end.

Tonight will be quiet—just me and my pump watching the State of the Union, praying for sleep. And giving thanks that we are inching closer and closer to the end of this difficult time.

Ashes to ashes. All things end. I'll receive that truth as a gift.

Songs in My Head

I Remember Singing
Thursday, February 14, 2013
4:12 p.m.

This morning I woke with Johnny Cash in my head, so as I shuffled into the kitchen in my plaid bathrobe, I tried to serenade Jim and Madelene on Valentine's Day, "Because you're mine . . ." But all that came out was a scratchy monotone, more sentence than song.

Sadly, one of the things that chemo has robbed me of is my singing voice.

But I remember singing. I remember singing the way I remember tasting food. I remember lots of things I used to be able to do. I remember walking with purpose. I remember sleeping soundly all night and needing no naps. I remember when my hands didn't hurt and my eyes didn't cross and my skin didn't peel. I remember having energy to burn, ideas that tumbled over one another. I remember working on important things with interesting people. I remember having things to talk about besides my health. I remember my old life, my pre-cancer life, though sometimes it feels as though that life belonged to someone else.

Sigh. Enough self-pity. It's an easy trap, like going down, down, down into Johnny Cash's burning ring of fire.

In fact, there is much to celebrate. I am now IV pump-free and can count seven treatments behind us. Though I'm still not very strong, I am much better than before, when I was receiving the full complement of chemicals. Dr. Reale promises that most of the side effects will diminish within a year of ending treatment, and some long before that. The oncology nurses high-fived and hugged me out of the infusion center in celebration of another successful treatment.

On a side note: walking into the cancer center is like walking into the TV bar Cheers. Everybody looks up from their work and calls my name as though they are glad to see me, as though I'm coming in for a beer at the end of the day. I'm waiting for someone to slip and shout, "Norm!"

Daily we receive letters and cards and e-mails of encouragement. I got a Valentine from ninety-year-old Este, who started her note, "Cancer is always a question." Indeed. We eat like kings. We are loved beyond reason. We have the finest medical care in the world. There are no storms on the horizon—literally or metaphorically.

So, for now, I must content myself with the memory of singing and feasting and sleeping and working and walking. We count on you to sing when we cannot, to eat with gusto, to sleep deeply, to work hard, to walk with a good, long stride.

As the days lengthen and the sun shines stronger, my hope for better days grows stronger, too. Thank you for sharing both the sunshine and the shadow. And for reminding us that soon, even this hard time will itself be nothing but a memory.

My Heart Is Not Here
Thursday, February 21, 2013
7:15 a.m.

My heart is not in Manchester today. It is in Georgia. I only wish my body were there too. Today longtime friends laid their twenty-two-year-old son in his grave after his unexpected death last week. We have spoken on the phone and been in touch by e-mail and letter. We have promised to be rocking on their front porch, sipping sweet tea as soon as we can. But that promise is small comfort, because we want to be there. Today.

But we can't. I can't travel. Neither my treatment schedule nor my diminished physical capacity makes it possible or wise for me to board a plane. A simple trip to the doctor's office or grocery store is a big outing for me these days. An out-of-state trip to a wrenching funeral would be my undoing. But our distance from friends in this time of desperate sorrow is almost more than we can bear.

I was afraid something like this would happen. Not that a friend's son would die—no one could imagine such a tragedy. But I was afraid that during cancer treatment someone we love would need us, and we wouldn't be able to be there. Many of the people we love live far from us—on another continent or another coast. When the reality of chemotherapy's rigors became apparent to me, I began to be afraid. What if something happened to our parents or siblings, an aunt or uncle, a niece or nephew while I was in treatment and unable to travel? Such worry is pointless and only creates more sorrow.

But still I worry. And I grieve.

Last fall, my gynecological oncologist warned that one of the most debilitating side effects of cancer treatment is grief. Grief over all the losses: physical, psychic, spiritual, financial, vocational, relational. "Go ahead and cry," he said. "You have a lot to cry about." So I do.

Today our hearts are torn. We would be in Georgia if we could. We are also mindful that today marks the first anniversary of a friend's death here in Connecticut: a remarkable woman cut down by cancer that gripped her hard and fast. Some days there are more tears than laughter in our house; today is one of those days.

But today, through the tears, we give thanks. It was a gift to have known these two wonderful people whose lives ended too soon. Today is a gift in itself, and not everybody gets a Today. And I give thanks for you, our friends and family who make the hard days bearable and the good days worth celebrating.

I am now a week out from treatment, regaining strength before next week's three-day cycle begins. The side effects that linger are irritating but inconsequential in light of the burdens others bear. I will live. Thank God, I will live.

Our hearts are torn but not irreparably broken.

VERSE 7

A Tea Party

MONDAY, FEBRUARY 25, 2013
7:44 A.M.

YESTERDAY AFTERNOON MY NEIGHBOR Anne called to invite Madelene and me to a tea party next Sunday afternoon. It is lovely to be invited. We drink a lot of tea at our house, but rarely is it accompanied by scones and watercress sandwiches and strawberries smothered in cream. I have fond memories of high tea at the Empress Hotel in Victoria, BC, where we have indulged a time or two. My friend's party will not be as delightfully *Downton Abbey* snobby as tea at the Empress, but it will be memorable in other ways.

This afternoon my friend will find out if the "irregularities" found in a recent CT scan are malignant or benign, if she is facing surgery or therapy or funeral planning. The tests that led to this shocking finding are part of her regular routine of CT scans every six months. You see, she is already living with cancer. Has been for seven years. And in those seven years of living with lymphoma, she has been diagnosed with three other cancers—all of which she has overcome. When they found an irregularity in last week's CT scan, she and her husband were struck dumb. Again? She cried for two days.

This afternoon, Anne will find out what "irregularities" means. She might be offered a diagnosis and treatment options. She might learn nothing. The oncologist may order more tests. She is seriously considering calling it quits, letting whatever this is run its course. Because she is tired. Tired of chemo and radiation and infusions and tests and surgery and weakness and disappointment and more cancer. Always more cancer.

But she dried her tears, took a deep breath, and, on the eve of a doctor's conversation that may change her life, decided to have a tea party. She's invited almost every woman she knows, all her sisters and her cousins and her aunts. And me, her sister in cancer.

Though it is a week away, I delight in anticipation of the dainty china tea cups, the lace doilies, the three-tiered sandwich selection. My friend, who knows that next Sunday I will still be crawling out of this week's treatment, told me that she will be happy to see me even if I'm in my Sick Sweater. "But I'll be wearing pearls," she said. "I may not get to wear pearls much longer."

I raise my almost-cold cup of Market Spice tea to her this morning, along with prayers for courage and clarity and peace. She is an inspiration to me and a reminder that there is always something to celebrate.

Hers is a response to sorrow my family has practiced for generations. We put the kettle on regardless of the day's news. When Trouble knocks, pour tea.

Verse 8

The Song That Doesn't End
Tuesday, February 26, 2013
6:12 a.m.

WHEN CLARA WAS IN kindergarten, one of her favorite TV shows was *Shari Lewis and Lamb Chop*. I have vivid, ear-painful memories of driving Clara and a carload of her Daisy Scout friends to a day camp, with them sing-shouting in the backseat, "This is the song the never ends! It just goes on and on, my friends." There is more, so much more to the song. And it never ends. Really. It never ends. Even now.

Today feels a bit like that song. My eigth treatment starts today, the first day of a three-day cycle. Will this ever end?

But Jim is home. What a gift. His plane landed in Hartford last night at midnight and even though a number of people have offered to retrieve him at the airport when he flies in late, I've given up sleep for Lent, so I did the driving myself.

We report to the cancer center at 10 a.m. Treatments are a bit shorter since they removed one of the chemicals from my cocktail, so we will be home well before dark. And Dr. Reale and the staff couldn't be nicer, so it will be a mostly pleasant day. Except for the reason we are there.

There is little else to report. Needless to say, I'm not really looking forward to what lies ahead.

But I woke up this morning to two things that have already set a new pace. My sister Carolyn forwarded a YouTube clip of My

Morning Jacket's Jim James singing his new song, "A New Life," on the *Jimmy Fallon Show*, complete with marching band, marimba, and orchestra. What a cool way to bop-she-bop into these early morning hours.

And I opened *The Hartford Courant* to this headline: "When Posts Cross a Line." A quick read revealed that it was not an exposé about a Post family reunion, but rather a controversy about posting news of the Newtown shooting on Facebook.

What a way to start the day: "The Song That Never Ends," "A New Life," and a headline that is funny only to me and the rest of us Post kids.

I'll be in touch at the end of the day. Thanks for singing this seemingly endless song with us. Same song. Next verse.

Still Singing It
Tuesday, February 26, 2013
5:37 p.m.

WE ARE HOME FROM treatment at the cancer center. To say that I am tired is a gross understatement. The weariness this evening is overwhelming. So, I have little news beyond that today's infusion was successful, that Dr. Reale is pleased with my general health, that two days from now the portable IV pump will be removed, that already side effects are re-emerging, and that I can't get Shari Lewis' irritating little earworm of a song out of my head.

Thank you again for your kindness, your prayers, your "go, girl!" encouragement. Through the weary fog, I remain grateful and humbled to be in your care. Though it seems this song will never end, I know it will. One day our songs will be all praise. But not yet. Not tonight. My hope tonight is that exhaustion translates into sleep—they don't always coincide.

I will write more once this three-day cycle is over, when we can count eight treatments behind us. Maybe I will have wakened a bit by then. Peace to you.

VERSE 8

Who Am I?

WEDNESDAY, FEBRUARY 27, 2013
2:31 A.M.

> Who am I? They often tell me
> I stepped from my cell's confinement
> Calmy, cheerfully, firmly
> Like a squire from his country house.
> Who am I? They often tell me
> I used to speak to my wardens
> Freely and friendly and clearly.
> As though it were mine to command.
> Who am I? They also tell me
> I bore the days of misfortune
> Equably, smilingly, proudly,
> Like one accustomed to win.[1]

AT THE RISK OF committing heinous hubris, I have to admit that this beloved poem, penned in prison by twentieth-century Lutheran martyr, theologian, and pastor Dietrich Bonhoeffer, is making more sense to me than ever before. Some of his words could be mine.

These months of illness and treatment have created an internal dissonance that continues to surprise me. There are many days when my current reality seems a foreign country, when the ways I used to think about myself no longer apply. I sometimes imagine that this is a dream from which I will soon wake, but you have to sleep in order to dream. Who am I? Sometimes I wonder. For example:

The insurance company has labeled me diseased and disabled. I am neither.

People tell me I look great. But I feel weak and pale and saggy.

---

1. Bonhoeffer, "Who Am I," 347–48.

I have tried to keep working on a writing project. On good days, I might write a paragraph or even a page that is carefully crafted and thought-provoking. But yesterday Jim found a yellow legal pad on which I had scrawled three words, none of which bore any relationship to the others or made sense to me. They were barely legible.

Food—both cooking and consuming it—has always been a great pleasure. I delight in a dark, round merlot or a smoky scotch, in flavor combinations subtle or startling and in desserts that tease the palate or warm the soul. But chemo therapy has rendered my taste buds "scorched earth," so now I eat because I have to, masticating only memories.

Sometimes I meet friends, colleagues, and family at a kitchen table or a favorite breakfast spot or in the grocery store or online. We talk about literature and theology and Scripture, culture and politics, vocations and vacations, family and friends, memories and wishes, grief and joy. Such conversations used to be everyday fare for me; now they are occasional at best. So, when we part, I am left alone to ponder great questions like "Where are my glasses?" I must make difficult decisions without wise counsel: NCIS or SVU, novel or newspaper, Chamomile or Sleepy Time, CNN or NPR?

My closet is stuffed with beautiful clothes and shoes enough to make a centipede jealous. But my daily wardrobe decisions are now confined to fewer options: sweater or sweatshirt, slippers or socks, flannel pajama bottoms or "big girl pants" (i.e., something in denim or corduroy and with a zipper).

I used to be a champion sleeper; Sunday afternoon nap was my best event. But now I shuffle off to bed every night knowing that the dark hours will find me wide-eyed and ruminating, occasionally accosted by an accidental hour's sleep.

I do not share these "disconnects" with you to garner pity or praise. But I feel that my temporary trouble has granted brief access to a world that for many is always confusing, frustrating, and disorienting, even frightening. What is it like to be permanently disabled or terminally ill? What of the falsely imprisoned, like Bonhoeffer? How does one overcome the deadly trifecta of poverty, violence, and illiteracy? Many are desperately lonely or awash in grief. Who are they? To themselves or to us?

I'm writing in the middle of the night because, as Sarah McLachlan sings, "sleep won't set me free."[2] But it has been a calming comfort to spend time with Bonhoeffer's poetry, so perhaps I will be able to snag an hour of sleep before day breaks. I leave you with the last stanza of "Who Am I?" hoping the words will bring you some peace as well:

> Who am I? This or the other?
> Am I one person today and tomorrow another?
> Am I both at once? A hypocrite before others,
> And before myself a contemptibly woebegone weakling?
> Or is something within me still like a beaten army,
> Fleeing in disorder from victory already achieved?
> Who am I? They mock me, these lonely questions of mine.
> Whoever I am, though knowest, O God: I am thine![3]

Another Checkmark
Thursday, February 28, 2013
3:09 p.m.

A couple of hours ago I was disconnected from the IV pump. That means that we have now completed eight of twelve treatments. I never dreamed we would get this far and still be able to stand.

We have a big weekend planned—big for me, anyway. Madelene is in a school play. I'm going to nap now so I can be awake and alert for opening night tonight. Clara is coming home for the weekend. We haven't seen her since Christmas, and I can't wait to

---

2. McLachlan, "Wintersong," (3:31).
3. Bonhoeffer, "Who Am I," 348.

lay eyes on her. These two "events" are more than I've done in a long time. And, if my energy holds, on Sunday afternoon I'll be at my friend's tea party.

Last night I was corresponding with a friend, telling him about plans for the last four treatments and beyond. He observed that this was the first time he had heard me talk about life after chemotherapy. I think that's a good sign.

Thank you, again, for your faithfulness to us. Jim has been doing a lot of "phone meetings" these last two days, and each conversation has started with concern for me, for us, for our household. At the grocery store this afternoon, the clerk's first question to me was not "Paper or plastic?" but "How are you?" I am touched by your kindness, surprised at how often you think of and pray for us, grateful for your support in these last months.

Today we are checking this eighth treatment off the calendar with deep gratitude and great hope. And a big yawn.

March Madness
Saturday, March 9, 2013
2:27 p.m.

IF YOU KNOW ME at all, you know that I know next to nothing about sports—can't tell a soccer ball from a shuttlecock. So, why "March Madness?" I'm not so interested in the basketball tournament coming later this month, an event that turns all of Connecticut into jargon-scattering, statistic-spewing, sleep-deprived sports crazies. (The Big East Men's Basketball Tournament is already keeping Nutmeggers up late, warming us up for the bigger tournament on the horizon.) I am living out a March Madness of my own, though some of the nonsense in my life is shared by others.

The snowstorm that was supposed to drop only a couple of inches of snow Thursday night dropped eighteen inches on our

Verse 8

neighborhood instead. Nobody was prepared for it. School was cancelled. Snow blowers were overheating, panting under the heavy load of snow. Our poor dogs are left circling and sniffing at snowbanks, anxious to get their business done. From the comfort of my kitchen, I watched our friend Sean doggedly shovel, blow, throw, and curse the snow in our driveway for three hours yesterday afternoon. Meanwhile, in Friday Harbor, Washington, where Jim's folks live, the daffodils are blooming. Crazy.

In an ordinary March, I would be fully occupied with Lent, Holy Week, and Easter preparations: crafting liturgies, writing sermons, preparing classes, making lists, spending time in prayer and silence, working the millions of details involved in this holy season. Instead, I have been sidelined by chemotherapy. My big hope is to get to worship tomorrow morning and maybe attend some of the Holy Week liturgies. It shouldn't be this way; I should not have this much time on my hands during Lent. Outrageous.

With every day that passes, I feel more like myself. Some of the side effects are easing. My energy level is a little higher. I actually slept some last night. Brilliant winter sunshine and fast-melting snow mean spring might actually arrive soon, which means the projected date for chemo's end is approaching. Here's the dumb part—I'll feel good just in time to go back into chemo on Tuesday. I don't know if these good days are reward for surviving chemo or if chemo is punishment for getting my hopes up. Ridiculous.

However, in the midst of all the madness this March, there is an "event" to which I look forward with great anticipation, almost as exciting as if UConn men's coach Kevin Ollie knocked on my door. My sister Janet is flying in from Texas on Monday to spend the week with me.

We won't stop talking from the moment her plane hits the ground until we hug before her flight home. In some families, conversation is like a chess game—one person talks while the other listens, then the other talks. It's sedate, respectful, calm, measured. But in my family, especially among us four sisters, conversation is more like flat track roller derby—fast, wild, and raucous. We jostle for the lead, step in front of and on each other, shout and laugh and cry and commiserate, and shove some topics out of the way, knowing we will pick them up on the next pass. We finish a conversation only to call back immediately with something we forgot to say. All we need are helmets and fishnet stockings, and the CT Rollergirls will be asking us to sign on for the season. That's a picture you don't want in your head.

For some, March Madness involves betting pools and uncomfortable stadium seats and overpriced T-shirts and lots of TV time. In our house this year, the madness is a lot less fun, way more expensive, and not even a little entertaining. But the snow will melt, the daffodils will bloom here too, and in seven-plus weeks, this round of chemo will be over and recovery will begin. At least, that's what I tell myself. The oncologist will be the one who decides.

I pray that the only things in your life that are crazy, outrageous, and ridiculous are the extent to which you are loved and cared for. Because that is the craziest part of all for us—the love and support and kindness and hope and prayer and encouragement you have poured into our lives is overwhelming, surprising, humbling, joyous.

Enjoy the ball games! We'll enjoy and endure our own March Madness right here at home.

Verse 9

Giving up Giving up
Tuesday, March 12, 2013
6:47 a.m.

When the alarm went off this morning, it seemed like a bad dream. Already? When I tried to wake the dogs to go for a walk, they just looked at me sleepily. Seriously? I started stumbling into my morning routine. And then I remembered that today is chemo day. And my heart sank.

For centuries people have "given things up" during Lent. Chocolate, coffee, fun, you name it. I am lately tempted just to "give up" for Lent. This has been a long road, littered with losses and disappointments, accompanied by a weariness that only deepens. Today I just want to give it up. Call the cancer center and say, "I'm done. I'm not doing this anymore."

Last night I had to take my wedding ring off because my hands continue to swell and burn and peel and ache. It means nothing—Jim and I still very married. But it was another loss, another sadness, another defeat. Today I just want to give up.

But I won't. Because I can't. And because I woke to notes from friends near and far. Because my sister Janet is here, who always makes me glad. Because my friend Lydia is going to visit us at the cancer center. Because tonight our friends Stephen and Karin will be at the door with love and supper. Because you give me courage and remind me that there is life waiting ahead.

On Sunday I wrote a long letter to our friends in Georgia—friends who recently suffered the death of their son. I offered them what I have already received from you. Prayers when they have none, a song when their hearts are silent, a hand when they stumble, a promise of love that even death cannot destroy.

So I will not give up. It would be foolish. More than that, you will not let me. And I will not give up because others, like our grieving friends, need me to keep praying and singing for them, reminding them of what you teach me. That we are not alone, that love is stronger than anything the world can throw at us, that one day tears will turn to laughter.

I have not given up my morning tea and newspaper, so I will take up those welcome disciplines now. And I will arm myself with your love, your prayers, your encouragement, your support. We really could not do this without you.

So I won't give up. I'll just give in—to another treatment, to another step on this unwelcome road. Thanks for walking it with us.

You Make Me Glad
Tuesday, March 12, 2013
7:11 p.m.

Janet and I got home from the cancer center around 3 p.m. Mercifully, treatment was uneventful. Dull is good. But instead of the mandatory nap time that was on the schedule, Janet and I sat in bed with rapidly-cooling tea and talked for two hours. It was more healing than sleep, I think.

Though I never look forward to chemo days or the two days of IV chemo at home, I always end these days with more joy than I felt when they began.

Verse 9

Four friends spent time with me at the cancer center —we talked and laughed and prayed. Our friends brought a lovely dinner and a big Royal Ice Cream cake, saying, "You need a party tonight. Here's the cake." Many of you write inspirational notes filled with hopeful reminders, fond memories, family wisdom, and potent bursts of love. And those who do not write continue to pray and remember us. And we can feel it around us, in us, over us, carrying us. All of this love and wisdom and hope and joy are so much more powerful than the temporary burdens we face.

So tonight, as we settle in with a big piece of ice cream cake I can't taste and a new episode of NCIS, I am glad. Grateful. Almost happy.

In the sleepless hours that lie ahead tonight, I will have many reasons to give thanks—and I will. And please remember to sleep well tonight—for me. Somebody ought to be enjoying the gift of peaceful slumber.

Another One Done
Thursday, March 14, 2013
2:49 P.M.

WE CAN NOW CHECK the ninth treatment off the list. Thank God. I had the pump removed at noon. Janet and I celebrated with lunch at Corey's Catsup and Mustard on Main Street. Then we stopped by Concordia so Janet could see the church building, and my friend and colleague Joshua met us there with hugs and encouragement.

Though there is more chemo ahead, it feels as though we have crossed a threshold of some sort. In fact, if the schedule holds, only three more treatments remain: nine days of chemo in all. I can survive that. I think.

I wish I had something profound or provocative to share, but all I can say is "Whew!" and "Thank you." It's time for a nap.

Addendum: As I lay down for the pseudo-sleep that passes for napping these days, I read a chapter of the novel that currently rests on the top of my reading pile. Before drifting off, I read this two-sentence image of a woman seeing a young neighbor off to war: "When I had to leave, she kissed me on both cheeks—a thing she had never done before—and said, 'There's just one thing to remember; whatever happens, it does no good to be afraid.' So I promised not to be afraid, and may even have been fool enough to think I could keep my promise."[1]

I suppose it's enough—trying not to be afraid.

Telling the Story
WEDNESDAY, MARCH 20, 2013
10:55 A.M.

ALMOST EVERY MORNING AS I boil water for my pot of Market Spice Tea, I think of Kenneth. Kenneth is long-dead; he was old when I knew him decades ago. When I first met Kenneth he told me the story that had defined his life: the story of his mother's death by fire as she fixed his oatmeal one cold winter morning. She was cooking over a wood stove while wearing a long-sleeved dress of some sort. Her sleeve caught on fire, and young Kenneth and his brother watched their mother burn to death while his father milked cows in the barn, oblivious to the flames consuming his world just across the farmyard.

Needless to say, I am cautiously conscious of the hot burner and its proximity to the sleeve of my bathrobe. And I remember Kenneth, whose life was defined by a tragic moment and the greater tragedies that ensued.

I read an article in Sunday's *New York Times* that has been simmering in my imagination all week. The article was called

---

1. Davies, *Fifth Business*, 57.

Verse 9

"The Stories That Bind Us." The author, Bruce Feiler, explains how sociological research into organizations and structures has led to thought-provoking discoveries in the field of family studies.[2]

Mr. Feiler and others have found that when families share a story—a defining narrative—the children of that family are better equipped to face life's complexities than children whose family has no story to tell. His research indicates that children who know their family story—the ups and downs, the joys and sorrows, the hilarious embarrassments, and the unspeakable tragedies—learn to fold their own joys and sorrows into that story. They survive, even thrive.

Since reading that article, I have been thinking about what I would do if I were preaching this Holy Week. My preaching would be informed by Mr. Feiler's research as it relates to the stories we will be telling during Holy Week, Easter, and Passover. We tell biblical stories of ups and downs, joys and sorrows, failures and successes, battles won and battles lost, death and life. And when we tell those ancient stories, we find our place in them and a place for all the defeats and victories we experience. When we tell those stories, we are reminded that no loss will destroy us and, equally important, that no success will last forever. We learn faithful endurance. And tempered joy. And great patience. And persistent hope.

I've also been wondering, as the weeks of my confinement continue, how the story of this unexpected time will be folded into my own small family's story. There have been sorrows, to be sure, but also unexpected pleasures and surprises. If Mr. Feiler is correct—if the biblical witness is true—this time of disease and disability and distance and dismay will make my family stronger for the telling, more ready for the next wind- or downfall.

And I've been thinking about Kenneth, whose father disappeared into alcoholism and whose brother was sent to an orphanage. One might expect Kenneth's story to be a "narrative of decline." But Kenneth was neither angry, nor depressed. He loved his wife and children with a quiet intensity. He was generous to a fault, sharing their meager blessings even when he and his wife

---

2. Feiler, "Stories That Bind Us," http://nyti.ms/17TFZmv.

had barely enough to feed themselves. Though unshed tears always brightened Kenneth's eyes and he missed his mother even eighty years after her death, the tragedy that defined his young life also informed his later years. He refused to let sorrow be the only story his children would tell.

I'm writing this morning. The sun is shining, melting the most recent snow. Friends have invited me for tea this afternoon. I am mostly able to keep my disappointment about my current situation at bay, but like Kenneth, the tears are never far away.

And it all gets folded into the story. I'm ready to turn the page on this chapter, but I can't just yet.

Verse 10

Falling and Rising
Monday, March 25, 2013
10:11 a.m.

We have recently been back in contact with a longtime friend who is, at this moment, keeping vigil with his dying mother. He has been keeping family and friends updated on his mom via Facebook, and in yesterday's posting added this from Julian of Norwich:

> If there is anywhere on earth a lover of God who is always kept safe, I know nothing of it, for it was not shown to me. But this was shown: that in falling and rising again we are always kept in that same precious love.[1]

As I steel myself for tomorrow's chemotherapy, I have been imagining a scene depicted so often in war movies—brave but frightened young men huddling in the trenches, awaiting the order to heave themselves over the berm and hurl their bodies toward the enemy, bayonets sharpened, guns blazing, death almost certain. Though my circumstance is nothing compared to that of soldiers in a war zone, facing this tenth treatment feels a little like that kind of entrenchment. One more time I will have to haul myself out of the relative safety of the trenches, knowing exactly what waits for me when I emerge. Not gunfire but chemicals. Not

---

1. Julian of Norwich. *Revelations of Divine Love*, 180.

danger but disappointment. Not blood but certainly sweat and tears. Not wounds but bone-deep exhaustion. Not death but halting steps toward life.

The mystic's image of "falling and rising" resonates with me today as it has not before. It is an apt image for those of us negotiating the undulating waves of illness and treatment. We fall and rise—too often, it seems—but always we are held in that precious love.

Today is a day to tie up loose ends and run errands before the coming three days of chemo and its attendant ills. More than that, today I remember our sister Ruth in her dying. I remember soldiers in dangerous places. I remember so many we love whose lives are hard. In this time of sorrow, in this Holy Week, we fall and we rise. And always, we are loved.

Who Knew?

Tuesday, March 26, 2013
7:24 p.m.

I CANNOT TELL YOU how much it means to know that you hold us in your prayers and in your thoughts and in your hopes. The Caring Bridge guest book entries of the last two days have brought me to tears. Your e-mails and text messages and cards and calls and the love we can feel across the miles are unspeakably precious gifts.

As the sun sets here in Connecticut, I find myself both profoundly grateful and completely exhausted. Treatment went well today—our time at the cancer center has been reduced from seven hours to four because they can push the drugs faster now than before. Dr. Reale and I had a first conversation about returning to my "old" life, and I am encouraged at his confidence in my relatively speedy recovery from this round of chemo. Two friends spent the day with Jim and me, bringing the world to our door. Sadly, I

Verse 10

missed Wendy's beautiful smile when she delivered dinner—I was still abed, sound asleep when she quietly knocked on the door.

The tears tonight are mostly for joy. Though I hate, hate, hate chemotherapy and the bi-weekly setbacks it brings, this time in our lives has been occasion for profound, unexpected experiences of community and care. As a friend often says, "Who knew?"

And who knew how exhausting this would be?

I wish I could describe the exhaustion to you. As is true for many of you, I have lived through tremendous physical depletion, emotional emptiness, and spiritual deserts. But the tiredness driven by chemotherapy is unlike anything I have ever known. Sometimes my legs just give out, and I have to clutch a counter or chair to remain standing. Sometimes I drift off mid-sentence, unable to conjure the next word. Too often I find myself sitting with my head in my hands, not from anguish but because it is simply too heavy. Hours pass with me just sitting, pretending to read while contemplating the backyard bird feeder. Jim can tell from my expression when the waves of weariness pass over me; he says my whole face collapses and the light goes out of my eyes. Ironically, this exhaustion does not always lead easily to sleep and sometimes even seems to prevent it. I don't tell you my sad story to garner sympathy or to say "poor me." Anyone who has walked this road before me might tell the same story. And though I have had six months to accommodate this weird weariness, it continues to sadden and surprise me. Who knew?

I imagine that this afternoon's death-like nap will preclude sleep in the dark hours. But this present darkness also brings much into sharp focus, especially during this holiest of weeks. There is much we do not know, but I know this with absolute certainty: we are loved deeply, ridiculously, completely, loved even to death. By God. By the One who gave his life for us that we might live. And we are loved by you.

Weary? Yes. Grateful? Beyond measure.

I'm going to pour a cup of tea, listen to a little more of Bach's "St. John Passion," maybe check out NCIS and *New Girl* on TV.

And then call it a day—a good day, a blessed day, a hopeful day. Good night.

Charity and Love
Thursday, March 28, 2013
3:57 p.m.

Today is Maundy Thursday, the first of the Great Three Days. On this night, Christians around the world will receive absolution for sin, wash one another's feet, and share the Lord's Supper. The chancel will be stripped of finery and the lights in the sanctuary dimmed. The liturgy this night is humbling and haunting, one of my favorites. But it's not a wild crowd-pleaser; nobody breaks down the doors to get in. I imagine the thought of dirty feet and final meals and bald-faced honesty about human depravity is less than appealing to many. Sadly, I will not be there tonight, either—I will not be among those whose sins are absolved, whose feet are washed, whose hunger is sated. But my absence from worship is not avoidance; it is the inability to be out and about tonight.

The IV pump was removed at midday today—the official end of the tenth treatment. Surprisingly, I am more tired and achy and weak and discouraged today than I have been to date. All of this is part of the chemo, I know, and all of this will pass. But it is a tremendous disappointment to stand on the doorstep of the Triduum and not walk through. I doubt I could even crawl through tonight.

Mercifully, when we cannot come to God, God comes to us. I have already been the recipient of Maundy Thursday charity and love. The nurse at the cancer center who removed the IV pump listened attentively to my sorrows, gently removed the bandages, made sure my prescription was ready for me at the pharmacy, and hugged me on the way out the door. Jim and I shared lunch after the pump was removed, and though I tasted none of it and ate only a little, we were together at the table, where disciples have always met. And I know that tonight, as my brothers and sisters in Christ gather in dark silence, the hand of forgiveness will rest on my sleeping head as well.

I am grateful to put this tenth treatment "in the rearview mirror," as my sister Mary says. I only wish I felt a little better, a little stronger, so that I could Easter with you in proper fashion or wish my Jewish friends "Chag Sameach" during their Passover celebrations. Next year, perhaps. In Jerusalem.

Thank you for your charity and love, and for sharing these Holy Week gifts with me and my family. I long to be with you in person, but for now, this will have to do.

Do Not Be Afraid, Stand Firm
Easter Sunday, March 31, 2013
10:13 a.m.

Jim and I were able to attend only part of last night's Easter vigil at a neighboring parish—my energy lasted only through the readings. My favorite of the six texts? The reading from Exodus, in which God routs the Egyptian army on the banks of the Red Sea. To be sure, it is a complicated story from a theological standpoint. Good for the Israelites but not so much for the Egyptians. I have heard the story a hundred times, but each time something new jumps out at me. This is what brought me to the edge of my seat last night: "But Moses said to the people, 'Do not be afraid, stand firm, and see the deliverance that the Lord will accomplish for you today; for the Egyptians whom you see today you shall never see again. The Lord will fight for you, and you have only to keep still'" (Exod 14:13–15).

I have typically rejected images of myself as a soldier in the war on cancer, as though I am embroiled in battle with a worthy opponent. But on this occasion, on this morning, with this text, the idea that God is fighting for me and subduing the enemy is enticing. And I cannot resist substituting "cancer" for "Egyptians" in this text: For this cancer that you see today you shall never see again.

Of course, the doctors have made no secret of the fact that the cancer I have is persistent. My gynecological oncologist describes it as "slow and indolent." I will be in testing or treatment for the rest of my life. But this particular season, this long Lent, this unwelcome, unexpected, sometimes hellacious season, will never be seen again.

Though some days are painfully long, in fact, the days of treatment are quickly passing. Soon I'll be plotting with parish leadership about my return to active ministry. Within months or weeks I'll be able to resume my life—social engagements, travel, community involvement, exercise, sleep. And on this Easter morning, I take comfort in God's words to Moses that soon the enemy will be vanquished, that this particular trouble will never be seen again.

I won't be worshipping in church this Easter morning—it would be too taxing, both physically and emotionally. Jim and Madelene are worshipping at Concordia. Clara is singing in the choir at Asbury First Methodist in Rochester, New York. I just finished wrapping small gifts for our Easter table. I would hide chocolate eggs around the house, but the dogs would consume them before anyone could find them. Now, in the silence of my house this lonely Easter morning, I'm going to sit down with the Easter gospel, mulling its promise.

And I'll add a few verses from Revelation: "Death will be no more; mourning and crying and pain will be no more, for the first things have passed away" (Rev 21:4).

And a last word from Exodus: "Do not be afraid, stand firm, and see the deliverance that the Lord will accomplish for you today; for the Egyptians whom you see today you shall never see again" (Exod 14:13).

Blessed Easter to you. Christ is risen. Risen indeed.

Verse 11

Right Now
Tuesday, April 9, 2013
6:42 a.m.

Julia's pumpkin bread and Anne Lamott's new book. Our parents' assurance of their daily prayers. Long conversations with Tim and Bob and Carol and Dave, some in person and some on the phone. Madelene's new prom dress hanging in the closet and walking the dogs on an almost-spring morning. These are such ordinary things, but in this season of my life, these are great and precious gifts.

Today we start treatment eleven of twelve. When I have energy enough to step back a bit, I realize that this is a great milestone and reason to celebrate. Almost done! But this morning, as I stare down both barrels of chemotherapy, I'm not in the mood for a party. Side-effects continue to linger and even grow as the chemicals sink their roots deeper into my system. I've got what Seinfeld would call "man hands." My whole body aches. My eyes don't focus properly, so Lord only knows what words I'm writing on this page. I can't taste a thing. Breathing deeply is a thing of the past. And sleep? I can barely spell it, let alone enjoy it. I tell people we are in the "teeth-gritting phase" of treatment. We just have to do it, whether we want to or not.

As you can tell, I'm having trouble getting distance on this process—it's always this way on the first day of treatment. In management speak, I'm letting the "immediate crowd out the important." I know that, but I can't seem to help it. That's why Julia's pumpkin bread made me cry. And why being able to shop for a prom dress with Madelene was so important. And why your love and prayers mean so much. Today I'm living in the "right now," and "right now" I hold on to the things close at hand—things I can taste and see and touch and hear in the moment. I hold on to you.

Through my self-pitying tears, I know that there is much for which to be grateful. This chemo season is, in fact, drawing to a close. We are loved beyond reason. And I am keenly aware that others' burdens are far greater than mine. I am particularly mindful of our colleague Bruce, whose life has taken a hard turn and whose "right now" is pretty bleak.

What's happening right now? Right now at my house the dogs are pacing in front of the patio doors, protecting us from those nasty squirrels. Right now Madelene is on the bus headed for school. Right now the newspaper beckons. And right now I know that, though I dread the treatment, this day will be filled with kindness and healing and reasons to laugh.

So I'll make friends with this "right now." What choice do I have? Pumpkin bread and hot tea. Your prayers to carry us through the day. It's a better day already than when it started.

We'll Be Alright
Tuesday, April 9, 2013
8:00 p.m.

AFTER A ROCKY AND reluctant start to the day, I'm alright now, past the despair of the "right now" that filled the early hours. Treatment today was pleasantly uneventful. Two friends kept us company. We had a wonderful conversation with Dr. Reale not only about treatment, but also about his work and the fiscal distress placed on cancer centers all over the country by financial decisions in

Washington. The side effects are settling in again, but I've been at this long enough to know what to expect. We got home around 2:30, and I was in bed and sound asleep within the hour.

The gentleman in the chair next to me received a lot of attention from the staff. I couldn't help but overhear some of their conversations. It seems that he and his wife had just moved to Manchester, midway through his treatment for cancer. You could hear the anxiety in their voices: starting over with a new medical team in a place where they knew no one. I'm adding him and his wife to my prayers tonight—prayers that they will be alright amid the wild changes in their lives.

The sun has set on what was the first real day of spring: seventy-five degrees, bright sunshine, gentle breeze. Linda brought a lovely dinner, though I was snoring when she knocked on the door. I am more at peace this evening, less anxious, resigned to what I know the next few days will bring.

I'm hoping to sleep, but if not, I have a lot to think about in the dark hours. Good things. Thank you—again—for your kindness to us. For your prayers, your posts, your patience with the wild ride this has been for us. We'll be alright. Good night.

Shakin' My Head
Thursday, April 11, 2013
1:45 p.m.

A LITTLE OVER AN hour ago, I was at the cancer center to have the IV pump removed, signaling the end of my eleventh treatment. I cried before we left the house—it's almost too much to believe that we are so close to being done with this round of chemo.

Our daughter Clara often jokes, "If you don't get your hopes up, you're never disappointed." This bleak aphorism is often accompanied by a favorite family whine, "I work in pain most of the time." And as our congregation's treasurer wryly cautions in months when the books are in the black, "There is no reason for immediate optimism." But I *do* get my hopes up, and I *don't* work in pain most of the time, and there *is* reason for optimism, and this season is fast drawing to its end. So today, we count eleven down and one to go. SMH ("shakin' my head" in text message dialect). How is this possible? It is almost more than I can believe.

One of the luxuries of this time has been the opportunity to read. I've picked up old favorites and tackled new titles and authors. Two days ago I finished Dave Barry's new book, *Insane City*. I am currently alternating between Anne Lamott's *Help, Thanks, Wow*, and Isabel Allende's *Paula*. Both are heartbreakers; I cannot read much of either at a sitting.

These remarkable authors and the wide array of literary styles in which I have been immersed have made me think more deeply about the power of writing. About why I write the stuff I do—the essays that beg a publisher, these entries in Caring Bridge, the scores of thank you cards I've written in these last months. As Allende says in her account of writing beside her daughter Paula's sickbed, which would ultimately become her deathbed:

> Writing is a long process of introspection; it is a voyage toward the darkest caverns of consciousness, a long, slow meditation. I write feeling my way in silence, and along the way discover particles of truth, small crystals that fit in the palm of one hand and justify my passage through this world.[1]

Thank you for reading what I write, for helping me find passage through this small, sometimes dark corner of the world. Knowing that you are out there as I grope to understand, as I struggle for patience, and as I give thanks for gifts that used to go unnoticed, is a tremendous gift to me.

Jim leaves for Chicago this afternoon. Madelene is staying after school for rehearsals. Our kitchen counter is dwarfed by an enormous basket of spring flowers delivered to our door yesterday.

---

1. Allende, *Paula*, 9.

VERSE 11

And now, with eleven treatments behind us and one before, I'll sit down for awhile. To read. Maybe to write. Or to nod off. This journey is almost at an end. SMH.

There Must Be Something to Celebrate
SUNDAY, APRIL 21, 2013
10:24 A.M.

MY DREAMS WERE ALL fear-based last night. Firefighters running into an inferno. Houses leveled by the blast. Runners hurled to the ground by a homemade bomb. Tanks rolling down city streets. Mangled bodies. Gun fights. Grieving families. Stone-serious police officers. It doesn't take a Jungian analyst to interpret these dreams. The last few days have been scary, as the whole country watched the explosion of a fertilizer plant in West, Texas, and the Boston Marathon came to a crashing halt.

Twisted around all those horrible dreams lifted from the newspaper I found more personal fears. What if my last chemo treatment is postponed? What if the scans aren't clean? What if the next round of treatment is not as manageable as I have been promised? What if the cancer returns soon? What if? What if? What if?

I am not one to be easily frightened. "Lions and tigers and bears, oh my!" was never my worry. But I realize that as this season of chemo draws to a close, I am afraid. Afraid of things that probably won't happen and, if they do, things I cannot control. Fortunately, the light of day and the encouragement of family and friends keeps me from seeing Edvard Munch's *The Scream* in the bathroom mirror. But, as many of you who live with cancer know, the fear is never far away.

In the midst of last week's horror, our friends John and Kristin sent us a bouquet of balloons. And not a small one—it was massive. There must have been two dozen or more brightly colored "event" balloons floating in our dining room. "Congrats 2002 Graduate." "Happy Anniversary!" "It's a Girl!" "Another Birthday?" "Get Well." Yellow smiley faces. The card attached to this brilliant cloud of ribbon, helium, and Mylar read, "We figure one of these holiday balloons should work!"

John and Kristin are exactly right. In spite of the fear in my heart and the terror around us in the world, there is always something to celebrate. These friends and scores of others have helped us maintain hope, have lightened dark days, and in this case, made us laugh out loud.

I told a friend this week that the "good weeks" are not as good as they were before—the chemicals continue to eat at my system and wear me down. But if I waited to do things until I felt completely well, I'd never do anything at all. So I'm well enough to have shared breakfast with a friend yesterday. Well enough to write a little. Well enough to do laundry and walk dogs and craft a beautiful spanakopita the other night. Well enough to go out to dinner with Jim Friday night, and even though I couldn't taste a thing, the food looked delicious.

As the last chemo treatment draws near, I am strengthened by your love, by my oncologist's confidence, and by these words, which were read at our wedding and will, one day, be read at my funeral:

> Do not fear, for I have redeemed you; I have called you by name, you are mine. When you pass through the waters, I will be with you; and through the rivers, they will not overwhelm you; when you walk through fire you shall not be burned, and the flame shall not consume you. For I am the Lord your God. (Isa 43)

Nobody promised us a danger-free life. Isaiah assumes floods and fires, fear and uncertainty. Twisted people plot terror in the streets of Boston while horrific accidents explode in small Texas towns. People of all sorts are diagnosed with cancer and worse. The question is not "Why does this happen?" but "How will we live in the midst of it?"

Verse 11

Thank you for your courage in the face of fear, your confidence when much is uncertain, your patience when things do not go as planned, and your encouragement that this hard time will pass. You have become teachers and models of faithful living in dangerous times.

In fact, we have much to celebrate. The balloons bobbing around our house are reason enough to be glad. Our joy is further multiplied by you.

Verse 12

Something's Coming

Tuesday, April 23, 2013
7:58 a.m.

What is the song in my head this morning, on the first day of the last treatment? This, from *West Side Story*:

> Could it be? Yes, it could.
> Something's coming, something good,
> If I can wait!
> Something's coming, I don't know what it is,
> But it is gonna be great![1]

Perhaps it seems a little odd that on this momentous day, a day for which I have waited with both dread and hope, I'm singing lyrics from a musical about impossible love and gang wars and punished dreams. But the song came to mind as our dog Maggie, the world's most chipper canine, came trotting into the kitchen at the sound of my spoon hitting the bottom of my empty cereal bowl. Every morning that sound is her signal to come lick the last of the yogurt and granola out of my bowl and then proceed to the dishwasher to pre-wash (i.e., lick) the dishes as they are stowed. Every day is a new day for a dog. And something good is always coming.

I've had a hard couple of days. The anticipation of today was overwhelming. When folks at both the bank and the grocery store

---

1. Sondheim, "Something's Coming," *West Side Story*.

yesterday gave me hopeful hugs, I burst into tears. I've been out of sorts, unpleasant to be around. I can't focus long enough to read anything of substance. As a friend quips darkly, "Let's hope the light at the end of the tunnel is daylight and not an oncoming train."

Though the next three days and a few after that will be ugly, by Thursday afternoon I'll be done with this round of chemotherapy. How is that possible? For six months I've been chained to chemo's calendar, haunted by side effects the oncologist has never seen before, and torn between discouragement and confidence, anger and hope. So, the thought that I might soon get my life back, that I might be able to work and travel and sing and taste and hike and sleep—it is almost more than I can bear.

It is hard to be sad for long when we have so much to be grateful for:

- My brother David calls the night before every treatment to remind us that we are always in his family's thoughts and prayers.
- My cousin Marilyn sent a lyric from the anthem her church choir sang Sunday: "Be still and know that I am God. Be still and know that I am here for you."
- Our friend Jeff writes from the rolling Wisconsin hills that "every storm runs out of rain."
- My friend Wendy got to Caring Bridge before I did this morning to leave a bright greeting; remembering her gorgeous smile is a welcome light on this dark day.
- Our friend Sharon walks this last treatment with us, all the way from Anchorage, guided by her own experience of this emotionally complicated event.
- We are flanked on either side by the world's best neighbors, who never fail to support and encourage us.
- Family and friends around the world daily remember us in their prayers and send love our way.

- Tomorrow my aunt Sandra has her last chemo treatment, the culmination of a year's journey during which she has been the model of hope and patience and confidence. She will walk away from a cancer that usually kills. She is a miracle.

And on this day, this unwelcome season in my life will soon end.

So, I'm singing as best I can, buoyed by hope that something good is coming. And grateful that lots of good things already have. Could it be? Yes, it could!

Oh Baby
Tuesday, April 23, 2013
6:48 p.m.

OH BABY, AM I tired tonight. Any relief I felt earlier about being close to the end of treatment is this evening eclipsed by noodly legs and running nose and blurred vision and tingling digits and exhaustion from the bone marrow out. This staff at the cancer center has been through this a million times, so, though they all knew this was the first day of my last treatment, they too are holding off their congratulations until Thursday, when the pump comes off. Then we'll be officially done, and the slow climb out of the pit begins.

We had a wonderful conversation with Dr. Reale about next steps. In two weeks I'll have a CT scan. The week after that I'll have the first of a six-month treatment with one of the drugs currently in my "chemo cocktail." But that drug has very few side effects, so soon I'll be planning a return to life, building the one-hour-every-three-weeks chemo infusions into my schedule. Dr. Reale said, "After what you've been through, you won't even notice this treatment." We'll see.

After treatment we called our parents, texted the girls, and then the dogs and I went straight to bed. I woke in time to enjoy a six-thumbs-up dinner from Lu-Anne and receive a beautiful bouquet of yellow roses from my sister-in-law Joanne. It was a lovely almost-end to a much-anticipated day. But the day isn't quite done—there's a new episode of NCIS on at 8 p.m., so I'll spend a little time with Agent Gibbs before calling it a day.

Thank you, again, for all your kindnesses to us. Your good humor, your deep confidence, your thoughtful words, and your steady presence in our lives have been gifts of incalculable worth.

We can now count the hours—forty-one—until this chapter of our life story is complete. I look forward to turning that page more than you can imagine. But not tonight. Not just yet.

Let Me Count the Ways
WEDNESDAY, APRIL 24, 2013
9:53 A.M.

"HAVE THE SIX MONTHS gone by fast or slow?" I get asked that a lot as friends and family help us make sense of recent changes in our lives. I think I'm still too close to this season to answer that question. In fact, some days I'm still struggling to come to terms with the fact that this is happening at all. It feels like somebody else's life, like a dream from which I cannot wake. But their questions get me wondering about how we will speak of these last months when they are far behind us.

Since the steroids prevent sleep, I have lots of time to ponder the takeaways of this season. Here is a brief list of ways we might approach that wondering from a statistical standpoint:

- ER visits: Two;
- Chemotherapy sessions: Twelve, each lasting three days;
- Chemicals infused with each treatment: Eighteen;

- Reading: Nineteen books, twenty-four issues of *The New Yorker*, two daily newspapers;
- Bouquets (fruit, flowers, balloons): Twenty;
- Number of days spent connected to chemicals: Thirty-seven;
- Meals delivered to our home: Forty and counting;
- Crossword puzzles completed: 150;
- Pots of tea consumed: 180 and counting;
- Frequent-flier miles Jim has accrued: 25,000;
- Expenses submitted to insurance company: $250,000 and climbing;
- Greeting cards received: A grocery bagful.

Some things are harder to quantify:

- Side effects: If alphabetized, the two-page list would look something like this:

    A: alopecia, allergies, appetite change
    H: hallucinations, headaches, hiccups

- Sleepless nights versus daytime naps;
- Vitals checks by nurses, lab techs, and physicians;
- Long walks the dogs were denied;
- Tears shed (for fear, sorrow, frustration weariness, gratitude, and joy);
- Forms signed, faxed, mailed, reviewed, and resubmitted;
- Decades of cancer research that have saved my life and millions of others.

Harder still, but more valuable by far, are those "intangible" gifts we have received from you. Your prayers and hopeful thoughts, the kindness from friends and strangers, the shoulders we have leaned on, the errands you have run, the visits in my home and at the cancer center, the wisdom shared by those who have walked this road before us, the burdens lifted, the hugs and kisses offered, the e-mails and text messages and phone calls and Caring Bridge posts—there is no way to number or assign a value to these. But these are the gifts that have carried us through this unwelcome season.

We are twenty-six-and-a-half hours from completing this treatment, but who is counting? Regardless of how we come to regard this season, I already know that all the memories will be infused with deep gratitude. Thank you, friends, for loving us beyond measure.

A Spring to Share
Thursday, April 25, 2013
10:50 a.m.

ONE HOT SUMMER AFTERNOON almost fifty years ago, I took it upon myself to pluck the snowy white blossoms off my mom's viburnum bush in the front yard and transfer them, one by one, into the dog house. I can still remember carrying those enormous blooms as carefully as though they were offerings to the gods. It took two of my pudgy little-girl hands to carry each one. I have no idea how long I worked at this pointless project, but when my handiwork was discovered, the dog was confused and my mom wore the tense jaw that marked a silence more damning than any punishment.

Why did I denude that beautiful bush? Why fill the dog's only safe place with wilting blooms? I have no idea, but it seemed like a good idea at the time.

And why, you are asking, do I remember that little episode today, on this last day of chemotherapy? Because yesterday afternoon we received delivery of three beautiful viburnum plants—gifts from my brothers and sisters to mark this new beginning, this long-awaited spring. I wept as they were unloaded from the car. To be remembered, to know that others are marking this day with us, to be reminded that life is already springing up around us is a gift too precious for words.

As I write, we have a landscaping crew here at the house doing the yard work I simply can't do this year: raking up the detritus of winter, mulching the beds, and coaxing grass from a lawn that sprouts mostly moss and dog poop. Tulips are opening. Trees are budding. The sun is warm on my shoulders. Spring has sprung. And just in time. Had this chemo winter gone on much longer, I don't know that I would have survived it.

In ninety minutes, I will be chemo-free, with my IV pump removed. My sister Janet said last night on the phone, "And you'll cry." I will. I cry about most anything. I cry at garage door openings. But this time the tears will be for relief and disbelief and hope. And gratitude.

This will be all the writing I'll do for today. After the pump is removed, Jim and I have a few errands to run, then we'll go to lunch and head home so I can crawl into bed and sleep. Or cry. Or read. Or, probably, just lie awake soaking up this amazing day.

We'll wait to plant the viburnum bushes until the landscaping crew has done its magic. Right now the plants are sitting in pots on the deck, absorbing last night's rain and this morning's sunshine, waiting for the first opportunity to explode into full life. And if, once they are planted and blooming like mad, some small neighborhood child chooses to pluck a blossom and take it home to her dog, it will be fine with me. Such beauty and hope and life can't be hoarded. This spring is meant to be shared.

Reprise

Sig
Tuesday, May 7, 2013
6:51 A.M.

He was a little boy doing his homework at the kitchen table, struggling with multiplication problems. He put his head in his hands and, exhaling deeply, said pathetically, "Heavy sig." His mother, washing dishes nearby, turned to him to ask, "What did you say?"

"*Sig*. Like in the books when someone is sad and they 's-i-g-h.'" She laughed, admitted it was a funny word and told him that though the "h" is silent, the "g" is too. And the "i" is long. Forever after, in his home and ours, disappointing or difficult moments have been greeted with a heavy "sig."

Ordinarily, we would be headed to the cancer center today for the first day of a three-day treatment. Mercifully, unbelievably, gratefully, that is not the case today. I am so glad those days are behind us. I no longer live under the sword of impending treatment and its accompanying sorrows. Instead, I get a mostly ordinary day, with the exception of a CT scan this afternoon.

I wish I could say the side effects are gone, but the chemicals don't know they're supposed to subside, so they keep digging in. Neuropathy, joint pain, sinus congestion, tastelessness, weariness—all these effects continue, and some are worse than before. But they will pass.

There are still lots of head-shaking moments. Our neighbor told me last week about a friend who, after similar treatment, saw marked improvement after three months and complete recovery after a year. A year?! Jim spoke with a colleague who survived colon cancer. She reported that when the chemo ended, her body rebelled with "We want the drugs!" and she spent a considerable amount of time in withdrawal. How it will go for me, God only knows.

We are starting to make plans for my return to full-time ministry. But all those plans are contingent on a clean CT scan, my tolerance of the next treatment that starts on Tuesday, and my general return to health. Dr. Reale is confident that the news will all be good. He's been a reliable witness so far, so I'm trying to trust him on this one too.

So, there has been no big sig of relief—just small ones. Will we ever breathe one great sigh? Will this unwelcome reality ever be completely behind us? Probably not. The task now is to live with the uncertainty but not be bound by it.

No other news here. We're still waiting for newly-planted grass seed to sprout. The viburnum bushes are flourishing on our deck. Much-needed rain will start falling tomorrow. Friends and family continue to shower us with love and hope and encouragement. And today, because there is no chemo, I can take my time with the newspaper and my morning tea. Small pleasures, but they all add up to deep gratitude and a blessed life. Little sig.

Still Singing
Monday, May 13, 2013
9:26 a.m.

Yesterday's preacher spent time with the Acts text, sharing the moving account of Paul and Silas "singing in the stocks" while unjustly imprisoned in a Philippian jail (Acts 16:16–34). We sang a hymn that continues to thrum in my heart and mind as I face the beginning of a second round of cancer therapy tomorrow:

> My life flows on in endless song; above earth's lamentation,
>
> I catch the sweet, though far-off hymn that hails a new creation.
>
> No storm can shake my inmost calm while to that Rock I'm clinging.
>
> Since Christ is Lord of heaven and earth, how can I keep from singing?[1]

How can I keep from singing, indeed? Though I do not relish what lies ahead, I know it cannot be worse than what has come before. And, more importantly, what lies ahead leads to life.

I see Dr. Reale tomorrow to learn the results of last week's CT scan and receive the first of a six-month series of treatments with Avastin, a ridiculously expensive miracle drug. Technically, Avastin (bevacizumab) is a "humanized monoclonal antibody" that slows the growth of the new blood vessels that might feed existing cancer cells.[2] My gynecological oncologist describes it as insurance—advanced additional treatment to stave off and possibly prevent a recurrence of the cancer. In spite of the expense and the risks and the disappointment of more treatment, this life is precious to me and worth fighting for. I am told that the side effects of Avastin are minimal, that I will be able to return to work while still in treatment. I pray that is true.

So, today I'm singing. And paying bills. And doing laundry. And running errands. A high school classmate is coming to visit on Wednesday—we have not seen in each other in more than thirty years. Madelene is in a high school musical this weekend, and late on Thursday night we will take in the new *Star Trek* movie. This

---

1. Evangelical Lutheran Church in America, "My Life Flows on in Endless Song," *Evangelical Lutheran Worship*.

2. Wang, et al., "Biological Activity of Bevacizumab," 335.

coming weekend I will undertake my first big outing since October, flying to Chicago for LSTC's graduation, fiftieth anniversary, and board meeting with Jim. I told Jim I'm eager to start being a "proper president's wife." He laughed—"proper" is not a word often used of me. This is a lot of activity for someone who, only weeks ago, struggled to climb the stairs. But I'm tired of being tired, so I'm going to push through the weariness and get back to living.

After all, if Paul and Silas can sing in a dungeon and believers all over the world continue to sing through imprisonment and hunger and war and violence and poverty, I can sing too. Though the tune is sometimes hard to hear and our voices tremble with tears, there is always a song to sing and someone close by to carry both the tune and the load. I trust today you will find the courage to keep on singing.

> The peace of Christ makes fresh my heart, a fountain ever springing!
>
> All things are mine since I am his! How can I keep from singing?[3]

Big News

Tuesday, May 14, 2013
1:37 p.m.

I thought the big news today would be the results of the CT scan. But I was wrong. The big news today is how deeply, relentlessly, and wildly loved we are.

This weekend was rich with gifts delivered to our door: a beautiful ripe fruit bouquet, a box of juicy chocolate-covered strawberries, a three-tiered petunia planter from the Sunday

---

3. Evangelical Lutheran Church in America, "My Life Flows on in Endless Song," *Evangelical Lutheran Worship*.

school children, and cards and calls and e-mails. I've always regarded Mother's Day as a day not only to thank our mothers, but also to delight in children. I am so grateful to be Mom to Clara and Madelene—they are astonishing gifts to me.

And now this.

I just returned from the cancer center to find a spring bouquet on my doorstep. But it was not just any bouquet from just anybody. This was a gift from Fran, who celebrated her hundreth birthday over the weekend. Fran, who is dignified and witty and beautiful and kind, sent me flowers to celebrate her birthday. Who would have imagined such kindness? How is it that we are so blessed to be loved by remarkable people like our girls and Fran and the Sunday school children and you? Words cannot express the humbling, joyful, head-shaking amazement I feel today.

My big news is tempered by the fact that just as I received the first dose of a stepped-down treatment, now that I have the rough stuff behind me, two other people began chemotherapy today at the cancer center. One, a man thirty years my junior, is receiving the same noxious chemicals I did. Another, a man my age who is recovering from surgery, now faces both chemo and radiation. I wanted to sit with them and hold their hands, tell them about the unexpected blessings that come in the midst of such harsh treatment. I wanted to assure them that although the hard news comes at you fast, the good news builds slower and lasts longer. I wanted to tell them that sleepless nights are pointless and to let the tears fall, because there will always be someone there to dry them. I wanted to tell them that life will be waiting for them when chemo is over. In other words, I wanted to tell them all the things you have taught me.

But I didn't. They were occupied with their own worries, their own sorrows, with their families clustered around them as mine was not so long ago, hanging on every word from the nurses, holding one another's hands, trying to be brave. They didn't need a visit from Happy Smurf. Not today.

So, after my own pointlessly sleepless night and a bucketful of anxious tears, I know again that love is real, that hope is possible, and that the joys always outweigh the sorrows. It is news worth repeating.

PS: The CT scan was clean.

Look for the Helpers
Monday, May 27, 2013
11:17 a.m.

Yesterday morning's preacher, my friend and colleague John, was reflecting on the disasters—both natural and human-made—of the last week and the questions such horrors raise for us. He told a story about his mother, who taught him how to face dangerous and frightening things. Rather than fixating on the dark of the sky or the power of the wind or the depth of the devastation, she advised him to do what Mr. Rogers has long recommended: "Look for the helpers."

John had other significant, thought-provoking reflections on the Trinity Sunday texts, but that simple observation has stayed with me. Last night when I could not sleep, I decided not to ponder the sorrow and surprise of these last months but instead to "look for the helpers." They are legion.

I found the oncology researcher at Mass General—a doctor I will never meet, but who is the world expert on appendicial cancer and confirmed my diagnosis. He described my situation in his analysis with this succinct first sentence: "This is a difficult case."

I found my nurse practitioner Karen Sullivan, my oncologists Phillip Roland and Michael Reale, and the scores of medical professionals and volunteers who have been God's hands of healing in my life these last months.

I found my family, both my small, immediate household and the broader household of my parents, siblings, cousins, aunts and uncles, nieces and nephews, and friends who are like family.

REPRISE

I learned from them about courage in the face of trouble, peace in the midst of danger, and strength in weakness. They taught us—again—about the power of love.

And I found you. I don't know if I have told you before, but Jim and I often had the sense—almost a physical feeling—of being carried by you and your prayers. My mother told me that one night during my treatment, she dreamt that Jim and I were being passed from hand to hand, as though by a bucket brigade, and that our feet never touched the ground. It really was like that, as you passed us prayer to prayer, lifting us day and night along the way.

I continue to gain strength every day. But I am often reminded of the significant neurological damage left behind by chemotherapy. Some of the side effects, which I thought had subsided, have reappeared. My fingers are swollen and sore, neuropathy plagues my hands and feet, I can't breathe easily, my sleep is disrupted, and my thoughts are sometimes jumbled. I have set two small June goals for myself. First, I will push my wedding band back on my swollen ring finger, and second, I will sing at full voice. Small goals, to be sure, but they would be great gifts.

Plans are underway for my return to active ministry in the middle of June. I may not be at full strength, but I'll do my best to be faithful to my calling and to the congregation and colleagues who have cared for and carried me for so long.

Another word from yesterday's liturgy has stayed with me: "[We know that] suffering produces endurance, and endurance produces character, and character produces hope, and hope does not disappoint us" (Rom 5:3–5).

Jim and I have swung wildly between emotional extremes; we have been tested and tempered by the obstacles thrown in our path; we have often been exhausted by the work required to heal. But I can say with all honesty that we have never been disappointed. Not by God. Not by our caregivers. And certainly not by you.

Because when I look for the helpers, I don't have to look far before I see you.

A Sign?

Tuesday, June 4, 2013
7:34 a.m.

As the memory of our long chemo winter continues to recede, I may have received a further sign that that dark time is really over. The Sick Sweater—my ratty, woolen cardigan companion through illness and self-pity—has suffered a setback. Though it has been washed countless times (Woolite only! Line dry!) without incident, when I pulled it out of the washer yesterday it was but a shadow of its former self. For some unexplained reason, the Sick Sweater has shrunk so that it is now better-suited to a runny-nosed toddler than a middle-aged woman with life-threatening cancer. I laughed when I pulled it out of the washer—perhaps the days of needing the Sick Sweater are really over!

In fact, I find myself looking forward more often than back. I had coffee with a colleague yesterday, and we didn't talk about cancer at all. Jim and I are eagerly awaiting the arrival of my sister Carolyn and her family from San Francisco tomorrow, and I know we will have lots of not-cancer things to talk about. I continue to inch toward a return to work in two weeks, modestly afraid that I won't be up to the task but itching to return to something that looks like "normal."

I receive the second Avastin infusion today, accompanied by none of the dread and fear of the first round of chemotherapy treatments. Rather than losing a whole day in The Chair and ending up as crumpled as an old sweater, I will be at the cancer center for only a couple of hours and leave strong enough to have a normal day afterward.

Thank you for your ongoing support and encouragement. We would not have survived the last difficult months without you. But just as it seems best to shove the Sick Sweater to the back of the closet, perhaps it is wise for us to push concerns about me out of the way as well, turning our attention instead to others who need our prayers and love.

So, even though I can't squeeze an arm into it, let alone my whole body, I will hold on to the Sick Sweater for a while longer. Today is lies limply on the drying rack—small, irrelevant, no longer useful, but a strong sign that it is now time to don not only new clothes, but also new dreams.

Moving Forward
Saturday, June 15, 2013
8:00 a.m.

I woke this morning realizing this is the last "Non-Sermon-Writing Saturday" I'll have. Hurray! I resume parish ministry on Monday and will be back in the pulpit next Sunday. Do you suppose I can still find my way through a text to put words together for a sermon? I fear my sermon-writing skills are rusty—it's been a full year since I last preached.

But we are gradually, gratefully, resuming something that looks like "normal." Ginger the golden retriever and I celebrated birthdays this week. She is older than me in dog years, but I have her beat in the wear-and-tear department. I've started physical therapy and am working to regain strength and flexibility after months of illness and inactivity.

Madelene finished her junior year of high school yesterday. She'll be spending the summer working on the trail crew for the National Park Service on Vermont's Green Mountain. She's also amassing hours behind the wheel in anticipation of getting her driver's license (and Clara's old car) in the fall.

Clara is in New York City this summer, singing with the Caramoor Center for Music and the Arts. She will move to Texas in the fall to sing as a young artist with the Fort Worth Opera. Ironically, she will be moving to Texas just as my sister Janet and her husband, Doug, leave Texas. They can honk as they drive by each other on I-35.

Jim is still commuting between Manchester and Chicago. He also has a fair amount of additional travel for the seminary this summer—to St. Louis, Pittsburgh, Portland, and Seattle, to name a few destinations. Fortunately, he will get to squeeze in a quick visit with his folks during the Seattle trip.

We are hoping to get all four of us to Iowa to visit family this summer. I haven't seen my parents since Dad's eightieth birthday party eighteen months ago. But, as with everything else, our travel plans were put on hold by the cancer diagnosis.

If anyone had told me a year ago that our lives would be so completely upended as they have been, I would have laughed out loud. No one could have anticipated the events of the last year—they hardly seem real to me, and I lived them. But the painful memories and middle-of-the-night tears and the random side effects are fading. Though I still can't taste anything and my hands are still too swollen to sport rings, these problems are insignificant compared with all that has been restored.

The rain has stopped here in Connecticut—at least for today—so we'll be doing outdoor projects. Within a few days, my life will pick up where I laid it down a year ago. Though I am not grateful for cancer, I am grateful for and humbled by all the good things that have come of this time—a keener sense of perspective about what matters, deep gratitude for unexpected and unmerited kindnesses, and the sure sense that love is more powerful than anything else in the world.

Postlude

An Ancient Song
Sunday, June 23, 2013
7:35 p.m.

Today, on my first Sunday back in the congregation after a year's absence, we marked the end of the long, dark year behind us with this ancient Jewish rite, the Birkat Hagomel, or Blessing of Thanksgiving. It is an ancient ritual required of all who have survived hardship.

Four categories of people are under ritual obligation to thank God for great kindness, using the words of the Birkat Hagomel:

- One who has crossed the ocean (e.g., an overseas flight)
- One who has crossed the desert
- One who has recovered from very serious illness
- One who has been released from prison

As I return to parish ministry following serious illness and a lengthy period of recovery, we decided, as a community of faith, to thank God in the way our Jewish ancestors have done for millennia. We offered this prayer as part of our opening rite to welcome me back into the midst of the congregation even as we acknowledged the suffering and healing common to us all.

This version of the Birkat Hagomel was brought to my attention by my friend and colleague rabbi Richard Plavin. It is adapted from a poem by rabbi Jennifer Bubitz.[1]

Birkat HaGomel (Blessing of Thanksgiving)

We pray to the source of blessing

for healing of mind,

healing of body,

healing of spirit:

wishing, hoping, begging

that it happen speedily, painlessly, and fully.

We pray that life should return to the way it was

before the illness, before the injury, before the brokenness.

Or we pray that healing come in different ways:

wishing, hoping, begging for relief, for release, for ease and liberation from suffering.

And what of that day, this day,

when that healing for which we wished, hoped, begged, prayed, becomes reality?

What words do we have to celebrate?

What words do we have to praise our source of blessing,

our source of strength, our source of healing?

We use these words, these ancient words.

This is our way of saying aloud, before God and one another:

we know you suffered,

we know you felt isolated,

we know your family and friends felt this pain, too.

1. Bubitz, "From Mi Shebeirach."

Postlude

We felt pain on your behalf.

And while we don't know exactly what it was like for you, from our own experience,

we do know.

And because we know, we're here now.

And we pray for you;

we give thanks for you;

we celebrate with gratitude the goodness bestowed upon you,

and we welcome you back into our midst, healed, or perhaps always healing.

And it will be our honor to respond to your blessing.

I offered the blessing:

Blessed are you, O Lord our God, ruler of the universe,

who rewards the undeserving with goodness,

and who has rewarded me with unmerited goodness and mercy.

The assembly responded:

May the One who rewarded you with all goodness and mercy

reward you with all goodness and mercy forever. Amen.

Bibliography

Allende, Isabel. *Paula: A Memoir*. 1st ed. New York: Harper, 2013.

Bonhoeffer, Dietrich. "Who Am I." In *Letters and Papers from Prison*, edited by Eberhard Bethge, 347–48. London: Touchstone, 1997.

Bubitz, Jennifer. "From Mi Shebeirach to Birkat HaGomel." *Ritualwell*. 2015. http://www.ritualwell.org/ritual/mi-shebeirach-birkat-hagomel.

Davies, Robertson. *Fifth Business*. New York: Penguin, 2001.

Eliot, T.S. "The Journey of the Magi." In *Collected Poems 1909–1962*. London: Faber & Faber, 1974.

Evangelical Lutheran Church in America. *Evangelical Lutheran Worship*. Minneapolis, MN: Augsburg Fortress, 2006.

Feiler, Bruce. "The Stories That Bind Us." *New York Times*, March 15, 2013, http://www.nytimes.com/2013/03/17/fashion/the-family-stories-that-bind-us-this-life.html?_r=1.

Hutton, Jeff. *Perfect Silence: A Novel*. Halcottsville, NY: Breakaway, 2002.

Julian of Norwich. *Revelations of Divine Love*. London: Penguin, 1999.

McLachlan, Sarah. "Wintersong." *Wintersong*. With Pierre Marchand, Diana Krall, Jim Creegan, Colin Cripps, Bill Dillon, Bob Doidge, Daryl Johnson, Brian Minato, Vince Mai, Ashwin Sood, Luke Doucet, David Sinclair, and David Kershaw. New York: Arista Records, 2006. Compact disc.

Perry, Michael. "O God, Beyond All Praising." Music composed by Austin C. Lovelace. Carol Stream, IL: Hope, 1982. http://www.hopepublishing.com/media/pdf/hset/hs_4462.pdf.

Sondheim, Stephen. "Something's Coming." Music composed by Leonard Bernstein. New York: Leonard Bernstein Music Publishing, 1957.

Vajda, Jaroslav J. "Before the Marvel of This Night." Music composed by Carl F. Schalk. St. Louis: Concordia, 1981.

Wang Y., D. Fei, M.Vanderlaan, and A. Song. "Biological Activity of Bevacizumab, a Humanized Anti-VEGF Antibody in Vitro." *Angiogenesis* 7 (2004) 335–45. http://www.ncbi.nlm.nih.gov/pubmed/15886877.

Watterson, Bill. *The Days Are Just Packed: A Calvin and Hobbes Collection*. Kansas City: Andrews & McMeel, 1993.

Wroblewski, David. *The Story of Edgar Sawtelle: A Novel*. New York: Ecco, 2009.

www.ingramcontent.com/pod-product-compliance
Lightning Source LLC
Chambersburg PA
CBHW071623170426
43195CB00038B/2070